LET MY PEOPLE GO!

USING HISTORICAL SYNCHRONISMS
TO IDENTIFY THE PHARAOH OF THE EXODUS

LET MY PEOPLE GO!

USING HISTORICAL SYNCHRONISMS
TO IDENTIFY THE PHARAOH OF THE EXODUS

Steven Collins, Ph.D.

Published by

TRINITY SOUTHWEST UNIVERSITY PRESS

PO BOX 91593 • ALBUQUERQUE, NM 87199

Trinity Southwest University Press
5600 Eubank NE, Suite 130
Albuquerque, New Mexico 87111

Let My People Go:
Using Historical Synchronisms to Identify the Pharaoh of the Exodus

By Steven Collins

Copyright ©2005 Steven Collins

Library of Congress Number: 2011941166
ISBN-13: 978-0615687940
ISBN-10: 0615687946

Printed in the United States of America.

Biblical passages are quoted from the *New International Version* (used by permission), the *New American Standard Bible* (used by permission), with many passages rendered from the original languages by the author.

DEDICATION

✍

For Danette

ABOUT THE AUTHOR

❧

Dr. Steven Collins has been researching and lecturing on the Bible and archaeology for more than 30 years. His broad formal training (University of New Mexico; Southwestern Baptist Theological Seminary; Luther Rice Seminary; International Institute of Human Rights, University of Strasbourg; Trinity Seminary; International Institute of Theology and Law; the College of Archaeology, Trinity Southwest University) and extensive experience in archaeology, anthropology, and biblical studies give him a commanding grasp of the issues involved in the investigation of ancient Near Eastern historical and scientific data relevant for understanding the Old Testament. He is presently Dean of the College of Archaeology, Trinity Southwest University (TSU—Albuquerque, New Mexico) and Curator of its museum collections. He has hosted and presented at each of TSU's International Symposia on Archaeology and the Bible since 2001, and is a dynamic lecturer regarding archaeology and biblical history at colleges, seminaries, and universities. He has also appeared in documentaries for the History, Discovery, and National Geographic channels. Prof. Collins is co-Director and Chief Archaeologist of the Tall el-Hammam Excavation Project (Jordan). His research, explorations and discoveries regarding biblical Sodom (Tall el-Hammam) are documented in a best-selling book co-authored with Dr. Latayne C. Scott, *Discovering the City of Sodom* (Simon & Schuster). He has also served as a Field Archaeologist for the Kursi, Bethsaida, and

Khirbet el-Maqatir excavations in Israel, and is a professional member of the American Schools of Oriental Research, Near East Archaeological Society, and the Society of Biblical Literature. In addition, he continues to travel extensively throughout Europe and the Near East in support of his research into the biblical world. From the banks of the Nile in Egypt to the Levant to the high plateaus of Asia Minor, he has meticulously pieced together the case for the historical veracity and authenticity of the Old Testament narratives. Prof. Collins has authored numerous scholarly papers, articles and books such as *Sodom and Science: The Application of Dialogical Methodology in Determining Material Correspondence between Archaeological Data and Biblical Narrative* (TSU Press), *The Search for Sodom and Gomorrah* (TSU Press); *Text and Trowel: A Handbook of Biblical Archaeology* (TSU Press); *The Defendable Faith: Lessons in Christian Apologetics* (TSU Press), and *Grasping New Testament Greek (*TSU Press).

TABLE OF CONTENTS

❦

TABLE OF TABLES

TABLE OF FIGURES

TABLE OF ABBREVIATIONS

AA   *Acta Archaeologica*

ABD   *The Anchor Bible Dictionary*

ACES   *The Australian Centre for Egyptology: Studies*

ANET   *Ancient Near Eastern Texts*

AUSS   *Andrews University Seminary Studies*

BAR   *Biblical Archaeology Review*

BASOR   *Bulletin of the American Schools of Oriental Research*

BRB   *Biblical Research Bulletin*

BS   *Bible and Spade*

CAH   *The Cambridge Ancient History*

DAE   *The Dictionary of Ancient Egypt*

ETS   *Evangelical Theological Society*

HZ   *Historische Zeitschrift*

ISBE   *The International Standard Bible Encyclopedia*

IEJ   *Israel Exploration Journal*

JATS   *Journal of the Adventist Theological Society*

JCS   *Journal of Cuneiform Studies*

JNES   *Journal of Near Eastern Studies*

JSSEA   *Journal for the Society for the Study of Egyptian Antiquities*

KMT   *KMT: A Modern Journal of Ancient Egypt*

MAA   *Mediterranean Archaeology and Archaeometry*

NEAEHL   *New Encyclopedia of Archaeological Excavations in the Holy Land*

NEAS   Near East Archaeological Society

NEASB   *Near East Archaeological Society Bulletin*

OHAE   *The Oxford History of Ancient Egypt*

OEANE   *The Oxford Encyclopedia of Archaeology in the Near East*

SAOC   *Studies in Ancient Oriental Civilization*

WA   *World Archaeology*

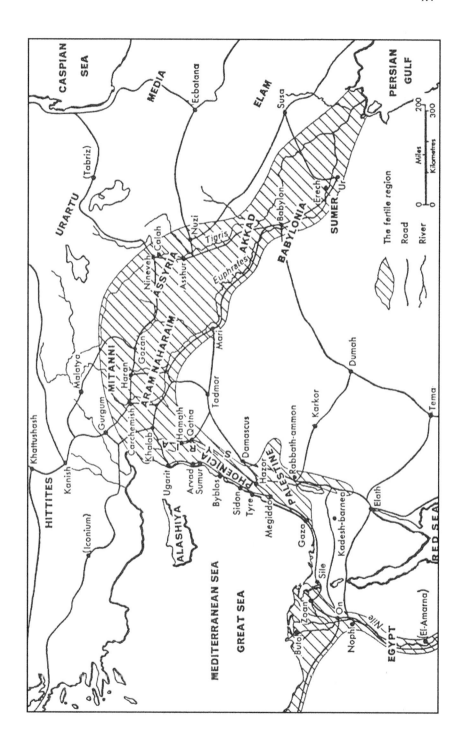

PREFACE

Bible students and scholars have a long history of speculation about the identity of the pharaoh at the time of the Israelite Exodus from Egypt. Indeed, we cannot help but wonder to which of Egypt's great kings Moses said, "Let my people go!" Some believe that the answer lies in comparing a selected biblical Exodus chronology (early or late) with a particular version of the Egyptian chronology (high, middle or low), thereby locating the Pharaoh of the Exodus at a point of chronological correlation. Thus, if the literal biblical date of the Exodus is said to be 1446 BCE, then we simply look at an Egyptian chronology to see who was ruling Egypt at approximately that date. Similarly, if the Exodus is thought to have occurred in the 13th century BCE, we only need to check an acceptable chronology to find out who was sitting on the throne of Egypt during that period of time. Beyond these approaches lie the theories of those who think that the whole of the Hexateuchal narrative is late Iron Age/Persian Period Judahite fiction or, perhaps, clever yarns of Jewish religio-political propaganda, or both. Such scholars do not believe in an Exodus event at all, so they would not event attempt to identify a corresponding pharaoh.

On the one hand, if we regard the biblical account of the Israelite Exodus from Egypt and its Conquest of Canaan as a reliable representation of these events, then it is reasonable to attempt to place those events within their larger ancient Near Eastern context, particularly with regard to Egyptian history. On the other hand, if the consequent impact upon Egypt (both stated and implied) due to the events of the Exodus cannot be approximately aligned with the known history of Egypt and the Levant, then surely the historicity of the Exodus and Conquest stories can legitimately be called into question.

It certainly follows that if the Exodus/Conquest events as described in the Bible do coincide with a commensurate portion of Egyptian/Levantine history, then the factuality of those events is raised to a reasonable level of probability. [It is beyond the scope of this study to determine such probabilities mathematically; however, this is possible given the number of potential points of correspondence between the biblical text and Egyptian/Levantine history.] It is the purpose of this study to suggest a placement of the Old Testament Exodus/Conquest narratives alongside a corresponding segment of Egyptian history during the Eighteenth Dynasty, whereupon an optimal number of historical synchronisms comes into view.

— Steven Collins, Ph.D.
College of Archeology
Trinity Southwest University

CHAPTER ONE

Approaching the Problem

—⟁—

S everal years ago, the museum where I serve as curator came into the possession of a small two-sided Egyptian seal. On each side was carved the hieroglyphic cartouche of an Egyptian king and a short message. At first glance, I thought the cartouche contained the prenomen of king Tuthmosis III, Menkheperre. Knowing also that several scholars had "nominated" him for Pharaoh of the Exodus, it really piqued my curiosity. However, I felt disappointed when I examined it more closely and re-read the inscription: "Menkheperure, son of Amun-Re," and "Menkheperure, king of all Egypt." Menkheperure was the prenomen for Tuthmosis IV, grandson of Tuthmosis III, son of Amenhotep II, and, based on my previous studies, one of the more unheralded pharaohs of the Eighteenth Dynasty.

The exploits of the great warrior-king Tuthmosis III and the vainglorious splendor of Amenhotep III, the "Caesar Augustus" of ancient Egypt, are well documented, but I confess that I knew very little about Tuthmosis IV other than what I had read from his Dream Stele, which was discovered between the paws of the Great Sphinx of Giza. I determined, therefore, to find out as much as I could about this Menkheperure. One thing led to another, and I ended up researching the entire Eighteenth Dynasty in order to learn more about the Pharaoh whose seal we were about to display in our museum.

But something else happened along the way: I became increasingly dissatisfied with existing theories about who might have been the Pharaoh of the Exodus. The more I reexamined the biblical accounts of the Exodus and Conquest, and the more I investigated the history of the Eighteenth and Nineteenth Dynasties, the more uncomfortable I became with the traditional identifications of the Exodus Pharaoh as Tuthmosis III, Amenhotep II, or Akhenaten from the Eighteenth Dynasty; or Rameses II of the Nineteenth Dynasty.[1] My dissatisfaction did not result from the typical disputes among early- (15th century BCE) and late-date (13th century BCE) Exodus advocates, nor from the many Egyptian and biblical chronology permutations suggested by scholars. My problem was with the fact that, regardless of which of the traditional suggestions was offered for the identification of the Exodus Pharaoh, virtually nothing in Egyptian history seemed to synchronize with the biblical account.

Then it occurred to me: given a generally-accepted lack of precision in both Egyptian and biblical chronologies, perhaps a strict chronological correlation is not the best way to proceed. Maybe the search for the Exodus Pharaoh is better served not simply by matching dates, but rather by attempting to align historical event patterns arising from the relevant biblical and Egyptian materials. Such materials could be analyzed and serialized separately, and then compared for pattern correlations, much like what is done with DNA "fingerprints." This kind of historical synchronism approach could also detect both "positive" and "negative" correlations in linear depictions of historical data in such a way that the positive data of the Exodus events from the Israelite point of view might correspond with negative data (events, propaganda, or even silence) from the Egyptian perspective. And because I could easily expand the range of potential correspondence—say, from the time of Jacob to the time of Joshua's Conquest of Canaan—an increase in the number of meaningful historical synchronisms over that longer period of time could raise the probability that a "match" has been achieved. So rather than merely linking up dates from selected chronologies (for example, the contention that since Tuthmosis III died in 1450 BCE, which is approximately

---

1   Such as A. Hoerth, W.H. Shea, and B.G. Wood (Tuthmosis III); C. Aling and C.C. Ryrie (Amenhotep II); the bizarre theories of E. Velikovsky (Akhenaten); and W.F. Albright, G.E. Wright, and K.A. Kitchen (Rameses II). See O. Zuhdi, "Dating the Exodus: A Study in Egyptian Chronology," *KMT* 4.2 (1993) 1527.

the time of the Exodus, then he must be the Exodus Pharaoh) I would look instead for synchronisms at multiple locations along the sequence of historical event patterns for both biblical and Egyptian history— theoretically allowing me to find the best overall "fit."

As far as the biblical text is concerned, I admit that a majority of scholars do not embrace its historical accuracy and authenticity as I do. So be it. But let me provide three areas of caution. First, evidence continues to mount in support of the contention that the Old Testament narratives mirror with great fidelity the ancient Near Eastern historical/ cultural contexts from which they allegedly derive. Second, if the biblical narrative—in this case from the time of Jacob to the time of Joshua—is not historically reliable to a significant degree, then the whole exercise of looking for historical synchronisms is useless. Third, our knowledge about Egyptian history will always be somewhat limited because objective, reliable ancient texts are practically nonexistent, though available documents do preserve a significant amount of historical information. Indeed,

> ...the vast majority of such texts surviving from Egypt were concerned much more with preserving and transmitting national traditions or with performing a particular religious or funerary role, rather than being attempts to present objective accounts of the past.[2]

In spite of the fact that the "historian who undertakes to write an account of the Pharaohs is soon aware that there is very little information available,"[3] there may be just enough data to make sense of the general picture. I do believe it is entirely reasonable to hold that both the Mosaic documents and the Egyptian texts preserve substantial amounts of historical information, although the Old Testament materials, in my opinion, are far more reliable at face value for historiographical purposes.

At best, the ancient Egyptians were accidental historians. Whether pharaohs or commoners, they never recorded the events of their lives with a view to providing future generations with accurate depictions of events as they unfolded chronologically through time. Far from it!

2   I. Shaw and P. Nicholson, "History and Historiography," *DAE* (London: British Museum, 1995) 130.
3   P. Montet, *Eternal Egypt* (London: Phoenix, 1964) xv.

While their personal experience and communication about their lives and times surely dealt with the realities they faced every day, it was primarily politics and religion that determined what they chose to record on papyrus and parchment, in wood and stone. As I. Shaw observes,

> The Egyptian sense of history is one in which rituals and real events are inseparable—the vocabulary of Egyptian art and text very often makes no real distinction between the real and the ideal. Thus the events of history and myth were all regarded as part of a process of assessment, whereby the king demonstrated that he was preserving Maat, or harmony, on behalf of the deities. Even when an Egyptian monument appears to be simply commemorating a specific event in history, it is often interpreting that event as an act that is simultaneously mythological, ritualistic, and economic.[4]

The operative word for virtually everything written by the ancient Egyptians is propaganda.[5]

As propagandists with the goal of fostering political stability and/or ensuring proper relationships with the spiritual realm, Egyptian writers filled their pages and monuments with descriptions of an idealized world conforming to their hopes and desires in every category of life. (Although this approach to "history" was typical throughout the ancient Near East, no other culture did it with quite the flair of the Egyptians.) Their method was to emphasize the positive (true or not) and expunge the negative. Thus, while Egypt has left us a magnificent legacy in its ancient texts, an accurate, detailed picture of what actually occurred in Egyptian history eludes us. Egyptologists have often remarked that there are few facts from ancient Egypt that can be known with certainty.[6] If the Egyptians have endowed us with some accurate historical accounts, it was not because they purposed to do so, but because the reporting of those events held propaganda value for them.

The Old Testament, given its penchant for brutal objectivity (see Appendix Three), stands in stark contrast to the propagandistic literary

---

4   I. Shaw, ed., *OHAE* (New York: Oxford University, 2000) 16.
5   See A. Gardiner, *Egypt of the Pharaohs* (London: Oxford University Press, 1961) 46-71.
6   B.J. Kemp, *Ancient Egypt: Anatomy of a Civilization* (London and New York: Routledge, 1989) 1-7.

genres of other ancient Near Eastern cultures.[7] Can you imagine the
fate of some priest or prophet of Amun-Re shaking an accusing finger
in the face of Rameses the Great and declaring, as the prophet Nathan
did to King David, "You are the man!"? The biblical narratives are
historiographical in nature, telling all—the good, the bad, and the ugly.
By contrast, what did the ancient Egyptians do when unedifying episodes
marred the record? They simply "fixed" their "history" by chiseling away
names, images, and inscriptions from monuments, temples, and tombs.
For example, witness Tuthmosis III's attempts to erase all remembrance
of his step-mother, Hatshepsut,[8] or Horemheb's efforts to eradicate the
memory of the Amarna Period pharaohs, especially Akhenaten.[9] Ancient
Egyptian regimes actively attempted to manipulate the perceptions of
both their public and their enemies regarding everything from Egyptian
affairs of state to a pharaoh's god-like persona. While the biblical writers
certainly had a socio-theological agenda, they did not afford their
characters the luxury of such purifying reconstruction.

　　Under these conditions, it is not surprising that scholars, including
those who take the Bible seriously as an historical document, have
found it difficult to place the biblical story of the Hebrew Exodus in
Egyptian documents. The Egyptians would never admit to the kinds
of events described in the book of Exodus. To admit such defeats and
weaknesses would have been to invite internal strife and territorial
rebellion. As a result, scholars seem always to have been at the mercy of
the most recently assembled chronologies, both biblical and Egyptian,
in order to fit the biblical Exodus scenario into Egyptian history. But
substantive associations between the two have proved difficult to
establish. Contradictions seem to emerge more often than not. Of course,
this could be due to the almost categorical difference between biblical
and Egyptian texts at the point of purpose and historicity.

　　For these reasons, the identification of the Pharaoh of the Exodus has
remained an ever-elusive goal. That is why I have attempted to utilize

---

7　　R.K. Harrison, *Old Testament Times* (Grand Rapids: Eerdmans, 1970) 19-25.
8　　W.C. Hayes, "Egypt: Internal Affairs from Tuthmosis I to the Death of Amenophis III," *CAH*
　　II.1 (1973) 318-319.
9　　J.E.M. White, *Ancient Egypt: Its Culture and History* (New York: Dover, 1970) 175-176. See
　　also D.B. Redford, *Akhenaten: the Heretic King* (Princeton: Princeton University, 1984) 223-
　　231.

historical synchronisms to locate the Exodus events along the continuum of Egyptian history. If both the biblical narrative from Jacob to Joshua and the Egyptian records from the Second Intermediate Period through the Eighteenth Dynasty can be taken at least somewhat seriously in terms of historicity, then it should be possible to see correlations between them, if indeed they were contemporaneous. Short of a time-machine, this seems to me to be the most reasonable approach available to us. And I think it yields some helpful results.

At this point, let me say a few words about five potential advantages of using the historical synchronism approach to identify the Pharaoh of the Exodus. First, it is simple and straightforward. Some historical synchronisms are obvious. In the light of the obvious, other synchronisms come into focus. With obvious and apparent synchronisms in view, additional synchronisms, including those involving what I call cultural specificity, become clear. And although the historical synchronism approach does not require the use of statistical analysis and probability theory in order to reach reasonable conclusions, it easily lends itself to such forms of analysis.[10]

Second, the historical synchronism approach incorporates a generally-accepted understanding of the biblical narrative as reasonably interpreted by most Old Testament scholars. Regardless of whether scholars believe the Hexateuch to be historical or fictional, there is virtual consensus on what the stories say. In other words, most scholars accept the stories at face value (i.e., they are in general hermeneutical agreement) despite the divergent theories of textual origin they may hold. The historical synchronism approach deals with what the stories say, explicitly and implicitly, and need not be a laborious hermeneutical exercise.

Third, it utilizes a reasonable understanding of Egyptian history already accepted by most Egyptologists. But I must qualify this point in view of what I have previously stated about the propagandistic nature of ancient Egyptian texts. Because there is often considerable doubt about the factuality of events recorded in Egyptian documents, the range of possible interpretations and resultant conclusions by historians can vary

---

10   P. Briggs, *Testing the Factuality of the Conquest of Ai Narrative in the Book of Joshua* (doctoral dissertation, Newburgh: Trinity Theological Seminary, 2001) 287-301.

significantly.[11] When this is multiplied by the same phenomenon in the Levant, Asia Minor, and Mesopotamia, it can be difficult to get a clear picture of what actually happened in the ancient Near East during a given timeframe. So I readily admit that the linear depiction of Egyptian history that I have presented for comparison with the Exodus events is necessarily selective on my part. However, I have tried to be as balanced and objective as possible and, in all instances, I have used reasonable interpretations and treatments of Egyptian events already stated and published by well-known Egyptologists and historians.

Fourth, the results of such an approach could serve as a corrective for both biblical and Egyptian chronologies. I have often thought of the biblical and Egyptian chronologies developed by scholars as two tall palm trees swaying side-by-side in the wind. If there was no wind, and both were standing perfectly straight, a mark on each tree at the twenty-foot level would remain exactly together. But when the wind blows, causing the trunks to flex and bend, the marks do not remain together even though they are both exactly twenty feet from the base of their respective trunks. Depending on the amount of sway and independent movement of each tree, sometimes the relative position of one mark seems to be above or below the other. But if the trees were bolted together precisely at the point of each mark, any remaining flexibility would be minimized and the trees would now essentially act as one. If the events of the Israelite Exodus from Egypt were "bolted" by historical synchronisms to the career of a particular pharaoh, variations in our construction of both biblical and Egyptian chronologies could be minimized, and our histories could be woven with greater precision and confidence.

Fifth, the approach is potentially applicable to other chronological coordination problems. As P. Briggs demonstrates in the development of his predicate criterial screening process for determining the factuality of ancient narratives, such as the Conquest of Ai in the book of Joshua,[12] it is possible to make correlations between narrative texts and their alleged physical environments, in order to determine whether

---

11 For example, some scholars state as fact the idea that Amenhotep's mother, Mutemwia, served as co-regent during the early part of his reign; others argue vehemently against such an interpretation. In Egyptian records it is often difficult to tell what is fact and what is bombast.

12 Briggs, *Testing* 219-221.

or not they qualify as true narrative representations.[13] Using historical synchronisms to correlate two separately derived yet related histories is a virtually identical process, which could potentially be used to solve similar chronological problems, not only between the Bible and its larger ancient Near Eastern context, but also between the chronologies of various ancient Near Eastern kingdoms.

Before moving on, let me make a few brief comments about cultural specificity, which I mentioned above. I define cultural specificity as elements of culture appearing in isolated time-space contexts. For example, certain ceramic forms (types) exist only in relatively short time windows, as do things like sickle swords and language dialects. The inclusion of culturally specific items in an ancient text can be a good indicator that such a written record belongs to a particular time-space context.[14] Indeed, to suggest that an author living in Egypt during the late Iron Age could (or would) write a story authentically set in the midst of Middle Bronze Age Canaan, replete with references to Middle Bronze Age customs and elements of material culture, would be ludicrous. Thus, cultural specificity applied within a context of historical synchronisms can increase the probability that a given text derives from a particular timeframe and not another.

13   See J.W. Oller, Jr., and S. Collins, *The Logic of True Narratives*, AMS/TSU BR.1 (2000); and S. Collins and J.W. Oller, Jr., *Biblical History as True Narrative Representation*, AMS/TSU BR.2 (2000). Brief versions of these monographs were also presented at the 2000 meeting of the ETS.
14   See K.A. Kitchen, *On the Reliability of the Old Testament* (Grand Rapids: Eerdmans, 2003) for an excellent discussion of historical synchronisms and what I call elements of "cultural specificity." See also K.A. Kitchen, "The Patriarchal Age: Myth or Mystery," *BAR* 21.2 (1995) 48-57, 88-95; and K.A. Kitchen, "The Patriarchs Revisited: A Reply to Dr. Ronald S. Hendel," *NEASB* 43 (1998) 49-56.

CHAPTER TWO

Will the Real Pharoah
of the Exodus
Please Stand Up?

—៣—

It is not my purpose to provide a detailed description and analysis of previous attempts to identify the Pharaoh of the Exodus, but merely to suggest the kinds of approaches and points of view that, in the past, have touched upon the problem. What will be immediately evident is that, regardless of the approach taken or the Exodus date adopted, general inconclusiveness still dominates the issue.

APPROACHING THE HEXATEUCH AS MYTH

One sure way to preclude the possibility of identifying the Pharaoh of the Exodus is to treat the Hexateuchal materials as myth. However, because such approaches are popular, I will briefly touch on them.

Narrative Embellishment of Historical Kernels

Early documentary theories regarding the development of the books of the Hexateuch and other Old Testament literature generally accept the idea that, although stories like the Exodus and Conquest narratives are encrusted with layers of legend and epic myth, most of them, at their cores, retain kernels of historical reality (not unlike the Iliad and other classical works). Such a view, however, makes it next to impossible to place the Exodus in any particular historical context, for the historical core elements of the story are often indistinguishable from layers of oral and editorial embellishment. Such an approach virtually precludes the possibility of discovering any connections between narrative text and material historical context, thus giving rise to all manner of speculations as to the literary evolution of the text itself. As K. A. Kitchen so aptly states:

> The theories current in Old Testament studies, however brilliantly conceived and elaborated, were mainly established in a vacuum with little or no reference to the Ancient Near East, and initially too often in accordance with a priori philosophical and literary principles. It is solely because the data from the Ancient Near East coincide so much better with the existing observable structure of Old Testament history, literature and religion than with the theoretical reconstructions, that we are compelled—as happens in Ancient Oriental studies—to question or even to abandon such theories regardless of their popularity. *Facts not votes determine the truth.*[15] [italics mine]

Creation of Fictional History (Emergence Theories)

Within recent years some scholars have rejected altogether the historicity of anything that purports to be Scripture of the pre-Iron Age. For them, "the world of the patriarchs is a fiction, not reality."[16] Even great biblical characters like Moses and Joshua are mythical creations "entirely divorced from historical reality."[17] There was no Israelite Exodus from Egypt. There was no wilderness wandering. There was no Conquest of Canaan. Instead, the people that later became the nation of Israel emerged from an autocthonous Canaanite population sometime in the early Iron Age (after 1200 BCE), carved out a kingdom for themselves in the central highlands, and eventually concocted a fictional origin and history for themselves, including everything at least from Genesis through Joshua.[18]

---

15   K.A. Kitchen, *Ancient Orient and Old Testament* (Chicago: InterVarsity, 1966) 172. For a masterful refutation of higher critical literary theories of Old Testament origins, see K.A. Kitchen, *On the Reliability of the Old Testament* (2003). In this work, Kitchen effectively destroys minimalist theories espousing late Iron Age origins of the Hexateuch and Judges.
16   N.P. Lemche, *Prelude to Israel's Past* (Peabody: Hendrickson, 1998) 39.
17   I. Finkelstein and N. Na'aman, eds., *From Nomadism to Monarchy* (Jerusalem: Israel Exploration Society, 1994) 13.
18   See N. Na'aman, "The 'Conquest of Canaan' in the Book of Joshua and in History," *From Nomadism to Monarchy*, Finkelstein and Na'aman, eds. (Jerusalem: Israel Exploration Society, 1994) 218-281. See also I. Finkelstein and N.A. Silberman, *The Bible Unearthed: Archaeology's New Vision of Ancient Israel and the Origins of Its Sacred Texts* (New York: Free Press, 2001).

CHRONOLOGICAL APPROACHES

For those who hold to the historical character of the early Old Testament books, attempts to identify the Pharaoh of the Exodus are mostly tied to chronological issues. The primary factor dividing the two major camps is the date of the Exodus itself. Without an approximate Exodus date, there is no hope of tying Moses to an Egyptian chronology.

Symbolic/Hyperbolic Approach (Late Date)

Because the Bible often gives numbers in nice, round figures, it is easy to construe them as symbolic or even hyperbolic. Although a good case can be made for the hyperbolic nature of at least some large numbers (in excess of 1,000) in the Old Testament,[19] smaller round numbers are also subject to varying interpretations. One such number is the 480 years mentioned in 1 Kings 6:1 which, at first glance, seems to be rather straightforward:

> Now it came about in the four hundred and eightieth year after the sons of Israel came out of the land of Egypt, in the fourth year of Solomon's reign over Israel, in the month of Ziv which is the second month, that he began to build the house of the LORD.

Some consider that stated numbers, like the 480 years (440 in the Septuagint) of this passage, should not be taken literally.

Period of 480 years (1 Kings 6:1) indeterminate. Advocates of a late date (13th century BCE) for the Exodus treat the 480 years of 1 Kings 6:1 as non-literal. With a firm 10th century date for the construction of Solomon's Temple as a starting point, just count backward—but how far?

A number of scholars[20] believe that the 480-year designation is actually a kind of numerical symbolism representing twelve generations, each generation being 40 years. But since an actual generation is more on the order of 25 years, the actual number would be about 300. Alternatively, why not use a 20-year generation, or even 30 years? The fact of the matter is that if you do not take the 480 years as a literal

---

19 See D.M. Fouts, *The Use of Large Numbers in the Old Testament* (doctoral dissertation, Dallas: Dallas Theological Seminary, 1992).

20 Kitchen, *Ancient* 72-75. Kitchen's view is typical. Cf. A.J. Hoerth, *Archaeology and the Old Testament* (Grand Rapids: Baker, 1998) 178-181.

figure, then the final number is indeterminate and open to a wide range of speculation.

Length of Egyptian sojourn indeterminate. It is interesting to note that most scholars who hold to a 13th century BCE Exodus, while not accepting the 480 years of 1 Kings 6:1 as literal, generally do accept the 430 years of Exodus 12:40 much more literally (see Appendix Two).[21] The reason is obvious: they face serious historical problems if they put Jacob and Joseph in Eighteenth-Dynasty Egypt. Therefore, they need all of those 430 years to get Jacob and Joseph safely (for their theories) into the latter part of the Middle Kingdom or the Hyksos Period where their stories fit much better. Thus, the length of Israel's Egyptian sojourn becomes rather indeterminate based on the needs of theories.

Length of Moses' life indeterminate. If the number 40 is thought to be a literary symbol for a generation, then should the 40-40-40 configuration of Moses' life also to be treated in the same manner as the 480 years of 1 Kings 6:1? This would mean that the 120 years of Moses' life according to Deuteronomy 34:7 was more on the order of 75 years—or 60, or 65, or 87, or 99. Obviously, if the 40-40-40 (120) years of Moses' life are not literal, then the length of his life is indeterminate and subject to myriad guesses.

Length of Judges period indeterminate. If the Exodus happened in the 13th century BCE, then a literal configuration for the length of the period of the Israelite Judges based on a face-value reading of the book of Judges becomes impossible. With this approach, whatever time elapsed between a late 13th century Exodus and the rise of the Israelite United-Monarchy automatically becomes the required timeframe for the biblical Judges. Thus, the length of the period of Judges is indeterminate.

"Pick your favorite pharaoh." If the smaller biblical numbers—480, 430, etc.—are indeterminate because they are hyperbole or numerical symbolism, then there can be no reliable way to track chronological precision between the biblical and Egyptian histories. As a result, the selection of an Exodus Pharaoh may owe more to subjective,

---

21   Ibid.

sentimental attachment than to historical evidence. In this case, Rameses II, for no particularly good reason, generally gets the nod.[22]

Literal Approach (Early Date)

What is meant by "literal"? Well, it could be that the 480 (Masoretic Text [MT])/440 (Septuagint [LXX]) years of 1 Kings 6:1 is exactly what it says, to the day; or it could be a rounded approximation. Perhaps the 40-40-40 (120) years of Moses' life is precise, or perhaps it is not exactly three periods of 40 years, but close. By all standards of chronological measurement applicable for discovering the Pharaoh of the Exodus, either of these approaches works; therefore, there is no need to belabor this point.

Period of 480/440 years (1 Kings 6:1) literal. Regardless of whether the 480/440 years of 1 Kings 6:1 is precise or a rounded approximation, those who ascribe to an early (literal) date for the Exodus place it in the midst of the 15th century BCE during Egypt's powerful Eighteenth Dynasty.

Length of Egyptian sojourn literal. There are two options as to the length of the Israelite sojourn in Egypt, from the time of Jacob until the Exodus. First, some argue in favor of a long sojourn (400+ years) based on the Masoretic Text of Genesis 15:13 and Exodus 12:40. Second, there are very good arguments in favor of a short sojourn (215+ years) based on the rendering of Exodus 12:40 in the Samaritan Pentateuch and the Septuagint, and supported by the apostle Paul in Galatians 3:1617. I admit that I strongly favor the second option (see Appendix Two).

Length of Moses' life (40/40/40 years) literal. If one takes 1 Kings 6:1 literally, then viewing Moses' life as approximately 120 years in length, divided into three periods of about 40 years each, is perfectly logical, and many scholars find no difficulty taking this approach.[23]

---

22   Kitchen, *Ancient* 57-59.
23   J. Finegan, *Handbook of Biblical Chronology*, rev. ed. (Peabody: Hendrickson, 1998) 224-245. Cf. E.H. Merrill, *Kingdom of Priests: A History of Old Testament Israel* (Grand Rapids: Baker, 1987) 57-91.

Length of Judges period literal. If the Exodus occurred in the mid-15th century BCE, then there is an abundance of time for all of the events in the book of Judges to take place comfortably before the onset of the Israelite United Monarchy.[24]

"Pick your favorite Egyptian chronology." By taking the "early date" biblical chronology, which places the Exodus events in the middle of the 15th century (ca. 1446 BCE), scholars who take this approach then select their preferred Egyptian chronology (high, middle, or low[25]), aligning an approximate date for the Exodus with a chronologically-close pharaoh from the Eighteenth Dynasty. The results are varied and rarely based on much more than chronological considerations: Tuthmosis III, Amenhotep II, Amenhotep III, or Akhenaten.[26]

Problems with Chronological Approaches

Approaching the issue of the Pharaoh of the Exodus merely from a chronological perspective has never produced more than a handful of casual suggestions. And pushing the flexibility of the 480-year approximation (1 Kings 6:1) beyond a few months or (at most) a few years yields little fruit. The fact of the matter is that neither the biblical nor the Egyptian chronology is able to be constructed precisely enough to allow either to be linked to the other on the basis of dating alone.

Egyptian chronologies. The Egyptians never intended to give us an accurate historical accounting of themselves.[27] And they have not. Because we must rely on documents that were originally written mainly as political, social, and religious propaganda, building a chronology of

---

24   See Merrill, *Kingdom* 141-188. See also R. Cate, *An Introduction to the Old Testament and its Study* (Nashville: Broadman, 1987) 228-230. Cf. J.M. Miller and J.H. Hayes, *A History of Ancient Israel and Judah* (Philadelphia: Westminster, 1986) 85-90.

25   See E. Wente and C. Van Siclen, "A Chronology of the New Kingdom," *SAOC* 39 (Chicago: Oriental Institute, 1977) 218; I.M.E. Shaw, "Egyptian Chronology and the Irish Oak Calibration," *JNES* 44.4 (1985) 295-317; K.A. Kitchen, "History of Egypt (chronology)," *ABD* Vol. 2, D.N. Freedman, ed. (New York: Doubleday, 1992) 322-331; and K.A. Kitchen, "The Historical Chronology of Ancient Egypt: A Current Assessment," *AA* 67 (1996) 113.

26   We *must* realize the lack of precision in the Egyptian chronologies on which we are accustomed to rely. Without greater precision, which is not likely to happen, a single candidate pharaoh cannot be identified with confidence based solely on chronological considerations.

27   This is not to say that we do not have a great deal of information from which to develop our histories of Egypt. We do. It is simply that the Egyptian concept of record-making and our concept of history are entirely different.

ancient Egypt is an intensively tedious task, to say the least. Arriving at a precise chronology is probably impossible. The further back one goes in Egyptian history, the less precision there is, especially considering the tumultuous intermediate periods for which most of the available information is hopelessly scrambled. The range of Egyptian chronologies formulated by recent and current scholars[28] yields a difference of up to fifty years from the lowest to the highest. Since ancient Egyptian history spans several thousand years, that range of deviation does not seem to be too significant. However, when trying to pinpoint the Pharaoh of the Exodus, even half that variance can mean a difference of one or two regnal periods.

Biblical chronologies. Deriving a chronology from biblical data seems rather straightforward. Of course, if one does not accept the historical veracity of the Old Testament, then fidgeting with the chronological details thereof is a meaningless exercise. But for those who do take the biblical text seriously and who also take a literal approach to the numbers involved, a reasonably tight chronology is possible.[29] However, the level of precision may still not be good enough to tie the Exodus events to the reign of a particular pharaoh. Thus, a purely chronological approach, even when fixed-date reference points (such as 966 BCE for the building of Solomon's Temple) are available, can only get us "in the ball park." And because both Egyptian and biblical chronologies are, to varying degrees, moving targets, using such an approach to identify the Pharaoh of the Exodus cannot yield a reliable result.

28   Kitchen, "Histoårical Chronology" 1-13.
29   Finegan, *Chronology* 224-245.

CHAPTER THREE

The Historical
Synchronism Approach

—⁓—

Because ancient dating methods were relative and event-based, often tied to the regnal years of kings with little concern for the kind of precision we desire today, it could prove helpful in searching for the Exodus Pharaoh to adopt a similar, event-based approach. After all, both the Egyptians and the biblical writers utilized relative, not absolute, dating in typical ancient Near Eastern fashion.[30]

For the current quest, an event-based methodology has several advantages over a fixed-date chronological approach. First, although it recognizes general chronological outlines and respects chronological boundaries as established by scholars working in the field, it does not seek—nor does it rely on—the attempted (artificial) precision of any particular chronology (high, middle, low, or otherwise). It thereby avoids the tedium that can lead to "not seeing the forest for the trees." Second, an event-based methodology (rather than one that simply looks at dates) concentrates on explicitly and implicitly predicted historical results and trends arising from event records preserved in biblical and Egyptian texts. Third, while chronological considerations tend to be somewhat two-dimensional and "colorless," event-based reckoning is able to appreciate and incorporate existing scholarly treatments and interpretations of both Egyptian and biblical history, including elements

---

30   See Finegan, *Chronology* 6-138; and E.R. Thiele, *The Mysterious Numbers of the Hebrew Kings* (Grand Rapids: Zondervan, 1983) 33-60.

of politics, religion, warfare, local and international affairs, architecture, society, and material culture.

I have called this event-based approach to identifying the Pharaoh of the Exodus the historical synchronism approach.

DEFINITION

Given two nearly parallel histories with numerous points of potential correspondence, an historical synchronism consists of an alleged fact or event sequence in each history, the existence of which is best or reasonably illuminated, explained, or comprehended in the light of the other. For example, the fact that the Sea Peoples, particularly the Philistines, did not settle along the Delta coast of Lower Egypt, but ended up colonizing the southern coast of Canaan, is historically synchronous with Egyptian accounts of the repulsion of the Sea Peoples by the maritime forces of Rameses III. The archaeological and biblical evidence that the Philistines did not, in fact, colonize the coast of Lower Egypt, but instead settled on the southern coast of Canaan, not only is synchronous with a particular segment of Egyptian history, but also serves to enhance the credibility of the Egyptian records of that period and vice-versa. In the case of the biblical accounts of the Israelite Exodus from Egypt and Conquest of Canaan—an historical record involving sequences of multiple events over a period of about fifty years—as the number of identifiable historical synchronisms in correlation with Egyptian history increases, so does the probability that the extant biblical record is factual.[31]

ASSUMPTIONS ABOUT
THE NATURE OF THE BIBLICAL TEXT

Every researcher who deals with the Bible operates from a set of assumptions (givens) that are foundational to the application of any research methodology. I have already stated that, based on substantial evidence, I accept the historical veracity of the Hexateuchal narratives. I also believe that they are divinely inspired. However, even if one does not accept these premises, the historical synchronism approach is still able to validate the authenticity of the Exodus narrative (and even a larger

---

31   Briggs, *Testing* 287-301.

portion of text, as we shall see). That a fictitious narrative written nearly a thousand years after the alleged events it describes could accurately parallel a modern construction of Egyptian history stretches credulity. As the old adage goes: if the shoe fits, wear it.

METHODOLOGY

The application of the historical synchronism approach to identifying the Pharaoh of the Exodus proceeds through five steps:

1. It is necessary to construct a serial history of the Exodus events as recorded in the Bible. I will begin with the time of Jacob and Joseph and proceed through the beginning years of Joshua's Conquest of Canaan.

2. Given a reasonable understanding and interpretation of the biblical text about the serial history drawn from it, there are (if the narrative is factual) explicit and implicit cause-and-effect relationships between what the biblical text states concerning the Israelite Exodus and the history of the associated Egyptian Dynasty. (I will dispense with the hermeneutical exercise of exegeting the biblical text because that has been admirably done by many commentators, most of whom would agree with my representation of the narrative.) In other words, if what is reported in the Exodus story actually happened, then Egypt would have been significantly impacted in predictable ways by such calamities as the Bible describes. The Egyptians, obviously, would not have elaborated on those damaging events, but it is quite probable that the larger picture of Egyptian history as we interpret it today, including the actions of its neighbors, would provide at least subtle indications of the deleterious effects of such events—plagues, plunderings, severe labor and military losses, the death of Pharaoh—regardless of the attempts of the Egyptian propaganda machine to cover them up. These explicit and implicit impacts of the Exodus events upon Egypt must be projected on the basis of a reasonable interpretation of the state of affairs in Egypt and surrounding regions during the appropriate period.

3. We must reconstruct a serial history of a commensurate portion of Egyptian history, paying specific attention to factors relevant for comparison with the biblical Exodus/Conquest scenario. There are only two possibilities to consider: the Eighteenth and Nineteenth Dynasties. I will only present a serial history of the Eighteenth Dynasty for two reasons: (a) the history of the Nineteenth Dynasty, particularly the reign of Rameses II, is not at all synchronous with the biblical record, as will become evident; and (b) as I proceed I will provide data from, and commentary on, the Nineteenth Dynasty to show why it fails to correspond with the biblical account of the Exodus.

4. I will superimpose the serial histories of the Israelite Exodus from Egypt and that of Egypt's Eighteenth Dynasty. If there are historical synchronisms shared between the respective serial histories, then at least some of them should be readily observable, even obvious. Other synchronisms may also become visible through a closer examination of relevant biblical and historical data, including elements of cultural specificity.

5. Based on the frequency of historical synchronisms arising from a comparison of biblical and Egyptian historical/chronological data, conclusions may be drawn concerning the plausibility of where we place the Exodus events in Egyptian history and the validity of the Exodus/Conquest record itself.

CHAPTER FOUR

The Biblical Component

—⁓⁓—

For the purposes of this study, particularly for references back to given points, I have enumerated the relevant biblical events, beginning with the times of Jacob and Joseph through the early years of Joshua's Conquest of Canaan (see Table 1). Also, I have divided the points in the summary into three sections: the *pre*-Exodus events (points 1 through 17); the Exodus *core events* (points 18 through 23); and the *post*-Exodus events (points 24 through 27).

Additionally, there are four reasonable assumptions that I will follow throughout:

1. Hexateuchal references to Egypt refer primarily, even exclusively, to Lower Egypt (the Nile Delta region) and not to Egypt in its entirety. There are several facts that support this assumption: (a) the early biblical patriarchs, such as Abraham, no doubt, had contact only with Lower Egypt, i.e., the region of the Nile Delta; (b) if Joseph and Jacob entered Egypt during the Hyksos Period—which I think is the most acceptable scenario in view of both biblical and Egyptian data[32]—then the Egypt of their stories was Lower Egypt because that was the epicenter of the Hyksos

---

32 Whether Joseph is placed in Egypt during the Middle Kingdom or the Hyksos Period does not matter for the purpose of identifying the Pharaoh of the Exodus. See my discussion in Appendix Two.

sphere of influence; (c) when Egypt was united under a strong cen-
tralized government, the two regions were always clearly delineat-
ed, with the king wearing *two* crowns, one of Upper Egypt and one
of Lower Egypt; (d) even when the Theban kings of Upper Egypt
ruled, they often preferred living in and reigning from their palaces
in Lower Egypt with its milder climate.[33]

2. Second, I assume a short sojourn of the Israelites in Egypt. As pre-
    viously suggested, while there are arguments on both sides of the
    issue, one of the strengths of the Septuagint (430 years in Canaan
    and Egypt, i.e., from Abraham to the Exodus) over the Masoretic
    Text (430 years in Egypt, i.e., from Joseph/Jacob to the Exodus) is
    the affirmation of the Septuagint computation by the apostle Paul in
    Galatians 3:16-17:

    > Now the promises were spoken to Abraham and to his seed.
    > He does not say, 'And to seeds,' as referring to many, but
    > rather to one, 'And to your seed,' that is, Christ. What I am
    > saying is this: the Law, which came four hundred and thirty
    > years later, does not invalidate a covenant previously ratified
    > by God, so as to nullify the promise.

All other things being equal between the long versus short Egyptian
sojourns, Paul's preference for the Septuagint rendering of Exodus
12:40 convinces me that the better option is the shorter sojourn—
about 215 years from Jacob in Egypt to the time of the Exodus.[34]
Computations relative to Exodus 6:14ff also tend to support a short
sojourn. Further, I think that the arguments in favor of Joseph serv-
ing as vizier in Egypt during the period of the Hyksos are stronger
than those placing his viziership in the Middle Kingdom.[35] (See my
discussion on the length of the Egyptian sojourn in Appendix Two.)

---

33 Most of the kings of the Eighteenth Dynasty spent a great deal of time in Lower Egypt and
    undertook many great building projects there. Recall Tuthmosis IV's "vision" near the Sphinx
    on the Giza Plateau.
34 However, a long Egyptian sojourn of 430 years does not impact the identification of the Exo-
    dus Pharaoh.
35 See J. Van Seters, *The Hyksos: A New Investigation* (New Haven: Yale University, 1966). The
    Hyksos were highly Egyptianized; their adopted culture would not have been appreciably dif-
    ferent from that of the Middle Kingdom.

3. The biblical documents are historiographically superior to the Egyptian materials from which our knowledge of Egypt's history is derived. Evidence forces me to view as suspect much of what we think we know about Egyptian history. Contrariwise, evidence compels me to accept the historical authenticity of the Hexateuchal narratives. Indeed, they should serve as a lens to correct, if possible, the "fuzzification" of a commensurate portion of Egyptian history.

4. I am assuming that the Pharaoh of the Exodus died in the *yam suph* ("sea of reeds") along with his entire army so that "not even one of them remained" (Exodus 14:28). The writer of Psalm 136:15 certainly understood the Exodus story that way: "[Yahweh] swept Pharaoh and his army into the *yam suph*." On the one hand, the need to propose a string of secondary and tertiary hypotheses in order to have Pharaoh survive the *yam suph* incident severely weakens any such theory. On the other hand, a straightforward reading of the relevant biblical passages supports that the Pharaoh of the Exodus perished along with his troops when the *yam suph* surged over them.

SERIAL SUMMARY OF THE EXODUS SCENARIO DERIVED FROM EXPLICIT AND IMPLICIT DATA IN THE HEXATEUCH

For the purpose of comparing the Exodus narrative with a commensurate portion of Egyptian history, I offer the following 27 points as a serial summary of biblical events (with dates using "biblical year" zero [=yb0] for the Exodus):

Pre-Exodus Events

Point One: Joseph is sold to Midianite caravaners and taken to Egypt where he becomes a slave. (yb-230) (Genesis 37ff)

Point Two: Joseph becomes vizier of Egypt, second administratively only to Pharaoh himself, and is introduced to the populace via a chariot processional. (yb-226) (Genesis 41:37ff)

Point Three: Due to conditions of famine in Canaan, Jacob and the Israelite tribes move to reside in Lower Egypt. (yb-217) (Genesis 47:9)

Point Four: Jacob stands before Pharaoh; the Israelite sojourn in Lower Egypt begins (see Appendix Two). (yb-215) (Genesis 47:7ff; Exodus 1:1ff)

Point Five: Joseph retires from his Egyptian viziership to live out his life with his people in Lower Egypt. (yb-208) (Genesis 47:27ff)

Point Six: Jacob dies and his funereal event in Canaan is attended by a large company of Egyptian officials. (yb-198) (Genesis 49:33-50:9)

Point Seven: Joseph dies and is given an Egyptian-style burial. (yb-147) (Genesis 50:26; Exodus 1:6)

Point Eight: The sons of Israel begin to multiply greatly. (yb-145) (Exodus 1:7)

Point Nine: A king arises in Egypt who does "not know Joseph." (yb-145) (Exodus 1:8)

Point Ten: The Egyptians apply a policy of hatred and persecution against a burgeoning Semitic population in the eastern Nile Delta region of Goshen (Lower Egypt). (yb-145) (Exodus 1:9)

Point Eleven: The Hebrews are conscripted, possibly enslaved, in order to build store cities (the names of which were perhaps later contemporized as Pithom and Raamses) for Pharaoh. (after yb-145) (Exodus 1:11)

Point Twelve: Despite their difficult servitude, the sons of Israel continued to multiply, so much so that the Egyptians are "in dread" of them. (yb-85) (Exodus 1:12)

Point Thirteen: The king of Egypt gives orders for the killing of male Hebrew infants as a method of population control. (yb-85) (Exodus 1:15ff)

Point Fourteen: Moses is born. (yb-80) (Exodus 2:1ff)

Point Fifteen: Moses flees Egypt into Midianite territory. (yb-40) (Exodus 2:11ff)

Point Sixteen: A king of Egypt dies while Moses is in Midian. (yb-10) (Exodus 2:23)

Point Seventeen: Under Yahweh's direction, Moses returns to the court of Pharaoh to demand the release of the Israelites from bondage. (yb-1) (Exodus 5:1ff)

Exodus Core Events

Point Eighteen: Ten successive plagues wreak havoc on Lower Egypt. (yb-1) (Exodus 7:14-12:34)

Point Nineteen: The Hebrews plunder Lower Egypt. (yb-1) (Exodus 12:35-36)

Point Twenty: Moses leads the Hebrew tribes and a host of other associated tribes (probably also Semitic) eastward out of Lower Egypt. (yb0) (Exodus 12:37ff)

Point Twenty-one: The Israelites camp between "Migdol and the sea." (yb0) (Exodus 14:2)

Point Twenty-two: The charioteer Pharaoh leads a sizable Nile Delta-based military force in pursuit of the sons of Israel. (yb0) (Exodus 14:5ff)

Point Twenty-three: The Egyptian forces, including Pharaoh himself, are drowned in the *yam suph.* (yb0) (Exodus 14:26ff)

Post-Exodus Events

Point Twenty-four: The bodies of the drowned Egyptians are recoverable from the shoreline of the *yam suph.* (yb0) (Exodus 14:30)

Point Twenty-five: The Hebrew horde, led by Moses, travels to Mt. Sinai to receive the laws of Yahweh; as a result of the subsequent Kadesh Barnea episode, they are directed by Yahweh to live as nomads in the wilderness for the next 38 years. (yb0) (Exodus 15:1ff; Numbers 13:1ff; Deuteronomy 2:14)

Point Twenty-six: Moses dies. (yb40) (Deuteronomy 34:7)

Point Twenty-seven: The Conquest of Canaan by Joshua and the Israelites begins. (yb40) (Joshua 1ff)

PROJECTION OF THE IMPACT OF
THE EXODUS CORE EVENTS UPON EGYPT

If the Exodus scenario presented in the biblical text actually occurred as stated without embellishment or exaggeration, then that series of events would have had a profound and devastating impact on Lower Egypt during the Eighteenth Dynasty. Additionally, given our knowledge of Egypt during the New Kingdom, events of this nature would have had predictable consequences for the Tuthmosid empire, particularly in contexts reliant upon Egyptian economic and military strength in the Nile Delta region. Several of the core events in the serial history presented above give rise to specific predictions about the consequences of such events for Egypt. Here I have focused on those core events. Later I will expand the discussion to include the remaining points (see Chapter Seven).

Point Eighteen: Prior to the Exodus, ten successive plagues wreak havoc on Lower Egypt. Although the Bible does not state precisely when this series of plagues began, it can be safely assumed that the entire period of plagues could have covered from several weeks to several months, or even years. Regardless, the cumulative impact upon Lower Egypt would have been devastating.[36]

The successive plagues are as follows:

1. Blood. The plague of blood made the water of the Nile (Delta) non-potable, and caused the fish to die.

2. Frogs. The plague of frogs was at least a great source of irritation, setting the people's nerves on edge.

---

36   It seems incredible to me that most scholars' discussions about the date and Pharaoh of the Exodus do not deal adequately with the inevitable impact of the Exodus events upon Egypt. In my opinion, it must be one of the key elements of the discussion.

3. Lice(?) gnats(?) mosquitoes(?). Whatever these tiny creatures were, they came in uncontrollable swarms over man and beast. One can only imagine the distress that resulted.

4. Swarms of insects (flies?). The plague of insects affected all the area of Lower Egypt except Goshen, where the Israelites lived.

5. Pestilence. This plague killed all the livestock in Lower Egypt; but the animals belonging to the Israelites were spared.

6. Skin boils/sores. This affliction of the most personal sort affecting residents of the Egyptian Delta increased their misery.

7. Hailstorms. The plague of hail severely damaged crops throughout Lower Egypt.

8. Locusts. What remaining crops the hail did not destroy, the locusts did.

9. Darkness. Whether this was a severe sandstorm or a supernatural blocking of light from the sun, it demonstrated the power of Yahweh over the chief Theban sun god, Re, or Amun-Re.

10. Death of the first-born.[37] The devastation and psychological depression brought about by the death of the first-born proved, indeed, to be the last straw.

As a result of the cumulative effects of these calamitous events, we must predict that Egypt would have suffered a severe economic setback in the region of the Nile Delta. No doubt, the plagues would have crippled the Delta economy for a considerable period of time due to population losses, including key administrative and military personnel, and pervasive crop failures (not to mention the disheartening of the general populace). By the end of the tenth plague, Lower Egypt would be teetering on collapse.

---

37 The term "first-born" may include the concept of the "primal son." For example, while it is doubtful that many of the pharaohs of the Eighteenth Dynasty were literally first-born, most were designated as the "primal son" and raised to become the next king.

Point Nineteen: Before they depart Egypt, the Hebrew clans plunder the wealth of Lower Egypt (at least the area surrounding Goshen). As if the plagues were not bad enough, Lower Egypt would have taken another major economic hit when the Israelites confiscated the personal wealth of its citizens (though some gave "voluntarily"). The biblical text suggests that the plundering was extensive. If this actually happened, then we could safely predict that Egypt's Delta economy would have been seriously impacted.

Point Twenty: A comparatively large number of Israelites, together with other Semitic clans and miscellaneous folk, depart Lower Egypt. Having already suffered through plagues and plundering, the Egyptian Delta economy would face the additional loss of a significant portion of its resident labor force. Surely, at this point, we would predict that any attempt at economic recovery for Lower Egypt would have been severely impeded.

Points Twenty-two and Twenty-three: Pharaoh, on his own chariot, leads "six hundred of the best chariots, along with all the other chariots of [Lower] Egypt, with officers over all…horsemen and [marching] troops" (Exodus 14:7-9) to pursue the fleeing Israelites. Subsequently, all of these Egyptian forces, including Pharaoh himself, were drowned in the *yam suph*. In one catastrophic moment, Egypt lost a significant portion—perhaps most—of its Delta military force, along with its king. The prediction here is obvious: Egypt would now face uncertain times, notwithstanding its remaining wealth and power.

Regardless of when these events are placed chronologically in the history of Egypt, there can be no escaping their impact. But since I have targeted the Eighteenth Dynasty as the most probable timeframe for the occurrence of the Exodus scenario, it must be pointed out that these calamitous events coincided with what is often called the Theban Supremacy or the Empire Period—roughly from the time of Tuthmosis I through the early reign of Amenhotep III. By far, Egypt had more to lose during this phase of the New Kingdom than at any other time. During this most magnificent era of Egyptian wealth, power, and prestige, the Black

Land had pressed an iron-fisted hegemony southward into Nubia and northeastward to the Euphrates River, extending its borders farther from its Nile core than ever before or ever after. If my assumption is correct that biblical Egypt is to be identified primarily with Lower Egypt, then the predicted impact of the Exodus core events upon Egypt as a whole would have even greater specificity in terms of the empire's ability to secure, control, and administer its Asiatic (Levantine) territories.

The logic is simple: Given that the Delta region in Lower Egypt was the only possible staging area for any commercial, military, and administrative operations in Canaan and Syria (i.e., biblical Canaan, "from the river of Egypt to the great river, the Euphrates," Genesis 15:18), Egyptian settlements and cities tended to be clustered along the Nile and only fanned out wider in the Delta region. Without both a vigorous Delta economy and a formidable Delta-based military force, Egypt would not have had the ability to extend its borders into the Levant, much less maintain its hegemony over those territories for any extended period of time. After all, the lands encompassed by Canaan and Syria were extremely difficult for any of the larger ancient superpowers to control, as G.S. Steindorff and K.C. Seele observe:

> In a land split by nature into so many unrelated divisions and so politically disunited, such an organization [as needed for comprehensive control of the Levant] could have been achieved only by a far greater employment of military and administrative force than was actually available to the pharaohs."[38]

Thus, there can be no doubt that Imperial Egypt's primary vulnerability, *vis-a-vis* its Levantine holdings, lay in the economic and military strength of Lower Egypt.

Had the biblical Exodus scenario occurred during the height of the empire—the middle of the Eighteenth Dynasty—we could only predict that its negative impact on the Delta region would have seriously threatened Egypt's ability to control its Asiatic territories. Such severe economic and military losses in Lower Egypt would have precipitated a

---

[38]   G.S. Steindorff and K.C. Seele, *When Egypt Ruled the East* (Chicago: University of Chicago, 1957) 103.

systemic, even if gradual, disintegration of Egypt's Levantine hegemony. Indeed, the existence and continuation of strong Egyptian control over Canaan (=Syria/Canaan) at any point in the Eighteenth Dynasty would signal that the Exodus core events could not yet have occurred. Had they happened, including the death of Pharaoh, then the erosion of Egyptian hegemony in Canaan would have immediately ensued. Even though the Egyptian administration—Upper Egypt being generally unaffected— would have acted to support its Delta economy and defenses, enough damage would have been inflicted that they would have needed a considerable period of time, even years, to begin to recover from both internal and northeastern territorial losses. As a result, the Levantine territories certainly would have become vulnerable to takeover by Egypt's rivals in northern Mesopotamia and eastern Asia Minor.

Before we examine the history of the Eighteenth Dynasty, I want to emphasize an additional point: Egypt's propaganda machine never would have admitted to any of these things. For Egypt to have advertised in any way that they had suffered such setbacks would have invited internal power struggles and rebellion in its provinces. Thus, the Egyptian records are not going to tell us anything about the negative effects of an Exodus-like scenario; at least, not on purpose. But I cannot help thinking that the over-all history of Egypt and its neighbors would somehow belie Egypt's attempts to expunge the knowledge of a biblical-style Exodus—and the Egyptians were very good at expunging.[39] On the one hand, if the Exodus core events had so dramatically affected Egypt, then it is almost unimaginable that their predicted results would not be visible somewhere in ancient Near Eastern records, even if much has not survived. On the other hand, if it is assumed that the Exodus took place during the mid-Eighteenth Dynasty, then the absence of explicit or implicit historical indicators (=historical synchronisms) suggesting the predicted effects of the Exodus scenario would surely militate against the idea that the Exodus took place during that period. And if there is an

---

39   Many of the monumental records of Egypt were defaced or destroyed in antiquity. Also, it was not uncommon for a king to usurp the monuments of his predecessors. Much of Egyptian history is difficult to reconstruct because of these practices.

absence of historical indicators supporting the existence of at least some of the predicted effects of the Exodus events, then that alone could call into question the historical veracity of the biblical record.

A Biblical Chronology of the Exodus Scenario
Taking a Literal Approach to the Old Testament
with the Exodus Date as Biblical Year Zero (y_b0)

y_b-**430**	Yahweh makes a covenant with Abraham (Gen 12.1-2; Gal 3.16-17)
y_b-257	Birth of Joseph (Gen 30.23-24)
y_b-229	Joseph in Lower Egypt (the Nile Delta region) (Gen 37ff)
y_b-226	Joseph becomes Vizier of Egypt (age 30); chariot parade (Gen 41.37ff)
y_b-217	Seven-year period of famine begins (Gen 41.54)
y_b-**215**	Jacob in Lower Egypt (age 130) (Gen 47.9)
y_b-**215**	Beginning of Israelite sojourn in Lower Egypt (Ex 1.1ff)
y_b-**210**	Seven-year period of famine ends (Gen 47.27)
y_b-208	Joseph retires his viziership (Gen 47.27ff)
y_b-**198**	Death of Jacob (Gen 49.33-50.9)
y_b-147	Death of Joseph (Gen 50.26; Ex 1.6)
y_b-145	The sons of Israel begin to multiply greatly (Ex 1.7)
y_b-145	A king arises in Egypt 'who did not know Joseph' (Ex 1.8)
y_b-145	Egyptian policy of hatred against Hebrews begins (Ex 1.9ff)
y_b-145	Enslaved Israelites begin to build Egyptian store cities (Ex 1.11)
y_b-85	Death of male Hebrew infants ordered by the king of Egypt (Ex 1.15ff)
y_b-**80**	Birth of Moses (Ex 2.1ff)
y_b-**40**	Moses flees Egypt into Midian territory (Ex 2.11ff)
y_b-10	The king of Egypt dies while Moses is in Midian (Ex 2.23)
y_b-1	Plagues against Egypt; Hebrews plunder Lower Egypt (Ex 7.14-12.36)
y_b**0**	Moses leads Exodus of Israelites from Egypt (Ex 12.37ff)
y_b**0**	Charioteer Pharaoh leads his army in pursuit of Hebrews (Ex 14.5ff)
y_b**0**	Nile Delta-based Egyptian forces destroyed in *yam suph* (Ex 14.26ff)
y_b**0**	Body of Pharaoh recoverable from shoreline (Ex 14.30)
y_b**40**	Death of Moses (Deut 34.7)
y_b**40**	Conquest of Canaan led by Joshua begins (Josh 1ff)
y_b**480**	Solomon begins to build the Temple (4th regnal year) (1 Kings 6.1)

Table 1.

CHAPTER FIVE

The Egyptian Component

—ɯ—

Comparing the biblical Exodus scenario with a potentially commensurate segment of the Eighteenth Dynasty requires the construction of a concise serial history of that period of Egyptian history. Unfortunately, the picture to be drawn is one of "impressionistic" generalities, not of "photographic" detail. Most of the Egyptian sources themselves are highly propagandistic and carefully designed to serve political and religious agendas. It often seems that while we possess a great deal of information, reliable facts are nonetheless in short supply. The early and late years of the Eighteenth Dynasty are, at best, shadowy. The affairs of the Empire Period are somewhat clearer, but far from perspicuous. To complicate matters, the historical interpretations of Egyptologists often differ dramatically.

Because of the aforementioned issues, I have determined that the safest approach for the purposes of this study is what might be called "reasonable historical averaging," i.e., the blending of historical constructions and interpretations that are already commonly accepted by Egyptologists. This avoids the extremes of some theorists, but considers that even middle-of-the-road Egyptologists spin their own radical views from time to time. I am the first to admit that significant variations can exist within an "average" range of historical interpretations. In such cases I have selected what I consider to be the most plausible options. Thus, while my brief serial history of the Eighteenth Dynasty may not

mirror that of a particular scholar, it is drawn from a reasonable range
of historical interpretations documentable from the works of a host of
notable Egyptological scholars.

SERIAL HISTORY OF THE EGYPTIAN EIGHTEENTH DYNASTY IN TERMS OF FACTORS RELEVANT FOR COMPARISON WITH THE BIBLICAL EXODUS/CONQUEST SCENARIO

For the purpose of comparing the history of Egypt's Eighteenth Dynasty
with events of the biblical Exodus, I offer the following 13 points as a
serial summary of the Eighteenth Dynasty (with dates using "dynasty
year" zero [=yd0] for the first regnal year of Amosis):

Point One: By the seventeenth century BCE, a long-lasting influx of
Asiatic Semites (probably Amorites[40]) into the Nile Delta region
culminates in the domination of Lower Egypt by the Hyksos kings
of the Fifteenth and Sixteenth Dynasties. Powerless to resist the
Asiatics, the Theban Seventeenth Dynasty often pays tribute to the
Hyksos regime,[41] which apparently has formed an alliance with the
Nubians to the south of the Theban realm.[42] (yd-100)

Point Two: After several failed attempts by the Theban Seventeenth
Dynasty to overthrow the Hyksos regime of Lower Egypt, a powerful Pharaoh named Amosis ascends to the Theban throne in the
early- to mid-16th century BCE. Amosis, the first king of the Eighteenth Dynasty, successfully routs the Hyksos from Lower Egypt,
reunifying the Black Land and reinforcing Egypt's eastern border
against further Asiatic incursions.[43] Having chased the hated Hyksos armies back to Canaan from whence they had originally come,
Amosis sets in motion a state policy of hatred against Asiatic Semites that becomes a standard for Eighteenth Dynasty administra-

40   Van Seters, *The Hyksos*. Cf. N. Grimal, *A History of Egypt* (Oxford: Oxford University, 1992) 185-186.
41   Ibid.
42   Ibid.
43   T.G.H. James, "From the Expulsion of the Hyksos to Amenophis I," *CAH* II.1 (1973) 293-296. See also D.B. Redford, *Egypt, Canaan, and Israel in Ancient Times* (Princeton: Princeton University, 1992) 125-129.

tions.[44] From this point on, the enslavement of Delta region Asiatics by the Eighteenth Dynasty is pursued with vigor, including incursions into the central hill country of Canaan to capture more slaves. As a result of this policy,[45] the population of central Canaan is severely depleted. But as would be expected, Amosis' primary focus is to increase the overall stability of Egypt through administrative, economic, and military development. (yd0-24)

Point Three: Upon the death of Amosis, his son Amenhotep I comes to the throne. Although early in his reign Amenhotep deals militarily with rebelling Libyans and Nubians, he spends most of his time refurbishing military garrisons and strengthening unified Egypt, continuing the patterns established by his father.[46] He dies childless. (yd24-45)

Point Four: Perhaps because of blood-ties to the Theban royal line, former general Tuthmosis I becomes the next pharaoh of the New Kingdom. Having quashed the customary provincial rebellions in Nubia, Tuthmosis turns his eyes toward the northeast, to Canaan and Syria. The anti-Asiatic (= anti-Semitic) sentiment established in Egypt by Amosis and continued by Amenhotep I also infects him.[47] With a now-formidable Egypt under his rule, his desire is to revenge the embarrassment of the Hyksos episode by making vassals of the Canaanite kings and expanding the borders of Egypt to the Mittani realm, if possible. He does reach the Euphrates River, but his visions of expansion are not entirely solidified.[48] In Tuthmosis' wake, the Eighteenth Dynasty now harbors an imperial lust centered on the intractable idea that its northeastern border must be the Euphrates.[49] Egyptian hegemony in Canaan has blossomed. (yd45-57)

---

44   Ibid. See also Grimal, *History* 193-195.
45   Most of the Eighteenth Dynasty pharaohs raided the central hill country of Canaan for slave labor. See R. Gonen, "The Late Bronze Age," *The Archaeology of Ancient Israel*, A. Ben-Tor, ed. (New Haven and London: Yale University, 1992) 211-257.
46   Grimal, *History* 202-206. See also James, "Expulsion to Amenophis I" 308-312.
47   Hayes, "Tuthmosis I to Amenophis III" 315-316. See also B.M. Bryan, "The Eighteenth Dynasty before the Amarna Period," *OHAE*, I. Shaw, ed. (New York: Oxford University, 2000) 230-235.
48   Ibid.
49   White, *Egypt* 165.

Point Five: Tuthmosis II takes the throne when his father Tuthmosis I dies, and he is immediately faced with territorial rebellions in both the Nubian and recently acquired Asiatic provinces.[50] Although able to keep the territories intact by launching at least one campaign into Canaan (perhaps as far as Syria) and another into Nubia, he is a frail and sickly man without a great deal of imperial fervor, often overshadowed by his queen, Hatshepsut. Under his rule, Egyptian hegemony in Canaan and Syria remains tenuous. He dies after ruling for only ten years.[51] (yd57-67)

Point Six: The death of Tuthmosis II initially brings uncertainty, mainly because his son and successor, Tuthmosis III, is too young to rule. Hatshepsut, the young king's step-mother, takes the throne and rules for about twenty years. A reasonably capable queen-pharaoh, Hatshepsut is able to keep the kingdom strong and maintains Egypt's hold on Nubia and the Asiatic territories, with many military campaigns undoubtedly being led by Tuthmosis III himself. However, the death of Hatshepsut is, perhaps, not accidental.[52] (yd67-88)

Point Seven: Whatever precipitates the death of Hatshepsut, Tuthmosis III claims his throne with a vengeance. The monuments and inscriptions of Hatshepsut are defaced or destroyed. Now in his twenties, Tuthmosis' bosom burns with the fire of his grandfather's imperial visions.[53] Faced with (the seemingly obligatory!) rebellions in Canaan and Syria, Tuthmosis determines to secure the Asiatic provinces via unprecedented military action. Arguably ancient Egypt's greatest general, and certainly one of its greatest pharaohs, Tuthmosis III tightens Egypt's grip on the Levant. His coffers are flooded with treasure. His courts receive dignitaries from virtually every land in the Near East. The Egyptian empire now reaches from the Euphrates in the north to the Fifth Cataract of the Nile in the south. At the time of his death, after ruling for nearly 55 years,

50   Ibid. 165-166.
51   Gardiner, *Egypt* 180-181.
52   Hayes, "Tuthmosis I to Amenophis III" 317-319.
53   Grimal, *History* 213-217.

Egypt is the richest and most powerful nation in the Near East and only getting stronger. (yd67-121)

Point Eight: A few years before his death, Tuthmosis III makes his son Amenhotep II co-regent, thereby ensuring a smooth transfer of power. Although Amenhotep is established on the throne of Egypt by the time of his father's death, the Egyptian provinces (particularly the Asiatics) launch their usual transition-period rebellions. But this time they have irritated the wrong pharaoh. Eighteenth Dynasty anti-Asiatic passions erupt from Amenhotep like a volcano. Known as a magnificent warrior who excels in archery and hand-to-hand combat—it was said that no other man could pull his bow[54]—Amenhotep II bears down on the Canaanite and Syrian princes with unparalleled ferocity. Crushing every enemy in his path, Amenhotep marches to the Euphrates River and raises a pillar to commemorate his military accomplishments, as his father, grandfather, and great-grandfather had done before him. In subsequent ceremonies, he personally beheads numerous captive Syrian chieftains and distributes their body parts to selected territorial cities as a warning. Needless to say, Egyptian hegemony over Canaan and Syria remains intact throughout the 26-year reign of Amenhotep II.[55] (yd121-147)

Point Nine: At the death of Amenhotep II, the Egyptian empire remains as strong and stable as ever. Although his successor, Tuthmosis IV, initially has to respond militarily to both Nubian and Syrian rebellions, the new king has a heretofore unseen weapon in his arsenal: diplomatic skill. As a young prince, Tuthmosis had earned a reputation as a courageous warrior—he had attained the title "Conqueror of Syria" even before he became pharaoh. Yet his much-publicized prowess as a master charioteer and archer is probably outweighed by his practical application of diplomacy, which proves to be his greatest accomplishment in terms of impact on the Egyptian empire.[56]

---

54   White, *Egypt* 168.
55   Grimal, *History* 217-220.
56   Bryan, "The Eighteenth Dynasty" 254-260. See also Bryan, *The Reign of Tuthmosis IV* (Baltimore: Johns Hopkins University, 1991).

Tuthmosis IV is well aware of two other ancient superpowers in his neighborhood to the north: Hatti (the Hittites) and Egypt's long-standing rival, Mittani. Surely Tuthmosis realizes that the Hittites would like to annex Syria—by now a perennial Egyptian holding—for its coastal access. He also realizes that Egypt's Euphrates border has always caused conflicts with Mittani. His answer: to make a "brotherhood" alliance with them. This accomplishes two things: first, an Egyptian/Mittanian alliance will reinforce the placement of Egypt's northern border in the vicinity of the Euphrates River and keep the Egyptians from having to battle Mittani again and again for control of the region. Second, the Hittites will not make a move on Syria as long as they face the combined military might of both Egypt and Mittani. The diplomatic skills of Tuthmosis IV pay off, and both of these goals are reached.[57] A true friendship develops between Egypt and Mittani, and the Hittites are kept at bay. As a result of these diplomatic maneuverings, Tuthmosis not only maintains the previously established borders of the empire, but also increases the prosperity of Egypt by eliminating the necessity of frequent military campaigns in Syria. (yd147-158)

Point Ten: Egypt under Tuthmosis IV remains the wealthiest and most powerful nation in the Near East.[58] The Egyptian realm ranges from the Fifth Cataract of the Nile in the south to the Euphrates River in the north. Egypt's northern flank is secured against Hittite incursion by the Egyptian/Mittanian alliance. All is well with the empire. As B.M. Bryan correctly writes, "It is presently impossible to prove that the Asian holdings of Egypt at the end of Thutmose's reign were not similar to those of [his father] Amenhotep II....his power in the far northern provinces was intact."[59] But suddenly, Tuthmosis IV is dead after a glorious reign of only about nine[60] years; in fact, the last documentable year for the reign of Tuthmosis IV is

57   One of the best treatments of Tuthmosis IV is found in N. Reeves, *Akhenaten: Egypt's False Prophet* (New York: Thames and Hudson, 2001) 43-52. See also Bryan, *Tuthmosis IV.*
58   R. Giveon, "Tuthmosis IV and Asia," *JNES* 28.1 (January 1969) 54-59.
59   Bryan, *Tuthmosis IV* 347.
60   C. Aling, *A Prosopographical Study of the Reigns of Tuthmosis IV and Amenhotep III* (doctoral dissertation: University of Minnesota, 1976) 2.

year eight.[61] Estimated to be between 25 and 28 years of age at
the time of death, his mummy reveals a healthy young man free
of dental wear, pathological indicators, and ante-mortem injuries.[62]
Additionally, the fashionable Tuthmosis is well-coifed, manicured,
and has pierced ears.[63] All of these factors indicate an untimely
death—a life cut short in its prime. And it is interesting to note that
at the time of his death, the otherwise-healthy Tuthmosis IV is "an
extremely emaciated man."[64] (yd147-158)

Point Eleven: Tuthmosis IV's military exploits into Asia are the last
of the Eighteenth Dynasty.[65] From the days of Tuthmosis I through
the reign of Tuthmosis IV, Egyptian domination over Nubia and the
Levant has reflected the superiority of Egypt's position in the Near
East during the Empire Period. W.C. Hayes clearly recognizes this:

> [The early Eighteenth Dynasty] picture of the military king
> is based chiefly on the career of Tuthmosis III, the years of
> whose independent reign were divided equally between his
> conquests abroad and his administrative tours....[It] is clear
> that the pattern of kingship followed by Tuthmosis III had
> already been established by his grandfather, Tuthmosis I, and
> was maintained, in so far as their abilities permitted, by his
> father Tuthmosis II, by his son and grandson, Amenophis II
> and Tuthmosis IV, and, in the early years of his reign, by his
> great-grandson, Amenophis III.[66]

Tuthmosis IV passes to Amenhotep III a magnificent kingdom, as
N. Reeves observes:

> Tuthmosis died unexpectedly, long before he could cel-
> ebrate his first sed-festival, or 30-year jubilee, and be-

---

61   See C. Aldred, *Akhenaten: King of Egypt* (New York: Thames and Hudson, 1988) 143-144;
      and Aling, *Prosopographical* 23.
62   G.E. Smith, *The Royal Mummies* (London: Duckworth, 1912/2000) 42-46; Cf. B. Brier, *Egyp-
      tian Mummies: Unraveling the Secrets of an Ancient Art* (New York: Quill/William Morrow,
      1994). Indeed, according to E.F. Wente of the Oriental Institute/University of Chicago, the
      most securely identified mummy among the Eighteenth Dynasty pharaohs is that of Tuthmo-
      sis IV; see E.F. Wente, "Who Was Who Among the Royal Mummies," *The Oriental Institute
      News and Notes* 144 (1995).
63   Smith, *Mummies* 42-46.
64   Ibid. 43.
65   G.W. Ahlstrom, *The History of Ancient Palestine* (Minneapolis: Fortress, 1994) 238.
66   Hayes, "Tuthmosis I to Amenophis III" 314.

fore, it is generally believed, the heir was of an age to be promoted as co-regent. Tuthmosis IV's skillful maneuverings had assured his son the inheritance of a 'great king': a land rich beyond compare, politically and administratively stable, and with borders stretching from Syria in the north to the fourth cataract of the Nile and beyond in the south.[67]

Nonetheless, as strong as the empire is at the end of Tuthmosis IV's reign, the accession of Amenhotep III to the throne of Egypt marks the beginning of the end for the Eighteenth Dynasty.[68]

During the first half of Amenhotep's long reign, residuals from the glory years of the empire propped up the administration of the kingdom, allowing it to operate reasonably well. Initially, because of his young age, Amenhotep's administration is handled by others. "It is probable," Bryan notes, "that Amenhotep III was a child at his accession," and that "his rule was conducted for him quite unobtrusively"[69]either by his mother Mutemwiya[70] or by other members of his family. From the very beginning, he seems ill-prepared to be pharaoh and has few of the military or administrative abilities of his Tuthmosid predecessors who had built the powerful Egyptian empire. Even after Amenhotep officially takes the reigns of the kingdom, his wife Tiy attends to the affairs of state.[71] She is capable and decisive, while he virtually retires to his own palace and pleasure bark, primarily in pursuit of beautiful women and sport.[72]

---

67   Reeves, *Akhenaten* 51.
68   The mention of Amenhotep III in the same breath with Tuthmosis III, Amenhotep II or
      Tuthmosis IV is hardly warranted. Although he inherits a wealthy and powerful kingdom,
      Amenhotep III is in no way equal to any of his predecessors. The fact that Amenhotep III has
      numerous large-scale building projects to his credit does not necessarily signal a healthy king-
      dom as some have tried to argue. Indeed, renowned Egyptologist K.A. Kitchen makes it clear
      that "In the formative years of empires, their energies go into territorial expansion; conspicu-
      ous display is expressed in major cities and monuments only later, often on the eve of decline
      or in its beginnings. A good example is Egypt...Amenophis III [Amenhotep III] saw the most
      opulence and new building [of the Eighteenth Dynasty], on the eve of decline, while the huge
      edifices of the [later] Ramesside kings accompanied that decline." See Kitchen, *Reliability of
      the Old Testament* 154.
69   Bryan, "The Eighteenth Dynasty" 260-261.
70   Grimal, *History* 221.
71   Ibid. 222.
72   Redford, *Akhenaten* 36-39.

Although Amenhotep III inherits the greatest world power of his day, he does little to preserve it. Indeed, as R. Giveon recognizes, his rule "heralds a weakening of Egypt's position in the world."[73] Further, A. Gardiner reminds us that "It is wrong to regard Akhenaten as the sole Pharaoh responsible for the loss of Egyptian prestige," for "Amenophis III was at least equally to blame."[74] The typical rebellions in the Nubian and Asiatic provinces draw a minuscule response from him. Unlike his imperial forbears, Amenhotep's colonial government is "lax in the extreme."[75] He fights a brief Nubian campaign, but launches no military operations whatsoever in order to secure the empire's Asiatic holdings—something every pharaoh has done successfully since the reign of Tuthmosis I more than a century before. From this point on, Amenhotep lapses into "the lethargic and voluptuous existence of an Oriental despot,"[76] degenerating into "a senile voluptuary"[77] who, for some unknown reason, is unwilling or unable to address the deteriorating situation in Egypt's Asiatic territories. But the situation is even worse than he thinks, for as J.E.M. White observes, "away to the north the storm clouds were gathering."[78]

As the long-but-feeble reign of Amenhotep III progresses through its fourth decade, the Hittite hordes, led by the mighty prince and soon-to-be warrior-king Suppiluliuma, loom beyond the western frontier of the Mittani Kingdom. They mobilize to seize the territory they have always desired: Syria and its seaports. For over a hundred years the Hittites have viewed Syria as a prized jewel, but could not avoid the reality of the Egyptian hegemony only recently strengthened by the Egypt/Mittani alliance forged by Amenhotep's father, Tuthmosis IV. As Suppiluliuma studies the situation, he seems to realize that Egypt, by the time of its transition from Amenhotep

73   Giveon, "Tuthmosis IV" 54.
74   Gardiner, *Egypt* 230.
75   White, *Egypt* 170.
76   Ibid. 169.
77   Ibid. 170.
78   Ibid.

III to Amenhotep IV, will not (or cannot) rise up to defend either its Asiatic territories or its Mittanian "brothers."[79]

After the death of Amenhotep III, in the early years of Amenhotep IV (Akhenaten), Suppiluliuma feels free to launch a major military campaign in an attempt to annex Syria, including attacks on Mittanian cities east of the Euphrates—all seemingly without any fear of Egyptian reprisal. Suddenly, all of the Egyptian and Mittanian lands west of the Euphrates are in Hittite hands. Local Syrian rulers, loyal to Suppiluliuma and backed by the Hittites, attack neighboring cities who beg Egypt for help. Their cries—mingled with those of Canaanite city-state princes—comprise the archive of el-Amarna. However, most of their letters go unanswered. The Amarna texts reflect a "weakening of Egyptian power, since the authorities were preoccupied with internal Egyptian affairs and give the impression that their interest in the land of Canaan had slackened."[80] A. Goetze accurately describes the situation:

> The advance of Hittite partisans as far south as the Biqa', the valley between Lebanon and Anti-Lebanon, and further east as far as Damascus ought not to have left the Egyptians indifferent; this was [traditionally] undisputed Egyptian territory. However, they either were unwilling or unable to help their friends in southern Syria. The letters of Akizzi [of Qatna]— like those of Rib-Adda [of Byblos]—are vivid testimony to Egyptian impotence.[81] [brackets mine]

From the final years of Amenhotep III through the early years of Akhenaten's reign, Egyptian hegemony in Syria ends as a result of Hittite aggression, and Egyptian hegemony over Canaan has

---

79   This fact is hard to imagine, but it is a fact nonetheless. By the early reign of Akhenaten, Egypt stands by and watches its closest nation-friend and northern ally, Mittani, as they are pummeled by the Hittites. Nor does Egypt lift a finger to save Syria from Hittite domination. We *must* ask, Why?

80   Y. Aharoni, *The Land of the Bible: A Historical Geography* (Philadelphia: Westminster, 1979) 170. See also S.D. Waterhouse, "Who are the Habiru of the Amarna Letters?," *JATS* 12/1 (2001) 31-42.

81   A. Goetze, "The Struggle for the Domination of Syria (1400-1300 B.C.)," *CAH* II.2 (1975) 16.

suffered nearly total disintegration. "Akhenaten, however," notes D.B. Redford, "had remained inactive through it all, as his northern border became destabilized; and rumor now had it that he *would not* act."[82] (italics his). Even Amurru has "broken away from the Egyptian empire, whose border now shrank back to south of the Eleutheros Valley."[83] Arguably, Egypt's position in the Near East has slipped from empire to nation. And the situation continues to worsen. (yd158-206)

Point Twelve: The decline of Egypt accelerates during the remainder of Akhenaten's reign. Seemingly powerless to respond to the continued cries for help from Asiatic city-state kings still clinging to Egyptian loyalties,[84] Akhenaten turns the Black Land even further inward upon itself in pursuit of quasi-monotheistic reforms—the elevation of the cult of the Aten—through which the traditional gods of Egypt are demoted, even persecuted. By the time Akhenaten dies, the Near Eastern political scene has changed dramatically from the days of the Egyptian empire as it had existed under the leadership of his grandfather, Tuthmosis IV. Without so much as a whimper from their Egyptian "brothers," the Mittanis, teetering on collapse after the first Hittite incursion, now crumble into utter ruin. Formerly, the Mittani Kingdom was second in power only to its ally, Egypt. Now Mittani is gone. The Hittites dominate the whole of Syria including the area of Damascus and now occupy first place on the regional power scale. With the Mittanis out of the picture, Assyria takes its place as "the second great power in the Near East."[85] Egypt, by far the world's mightiest nation only a few decades earlier, now ranks third in power behind Hatti and Assyria. (yd196-213)

---

82   Redford, *Egypt, Canaan* 176. See also T. Bryce, *The Kingdom of the Hittites* (Oxford: Oxford University Press, 1998) 174-193, who clearly points out the impotence of Akhenaten to act in the face of Hittite aggression. Egypt made numerous threats, but was never able to back them up with any kind of military response.
83   Ibid. 177.
84   Some believe that the el-Amarna correspondence reflects the routine operations of the Egyptian empire in Asia. But I think that cannot be the case. See my comments in note 115.
85   G. Roux, *Ancient Iraq*, third ed. (New York: Penguin, 1992) 260-261.

Point Thirteen: "By the middle of the fourteenth century B.C.," states Redford, "the Eighteenth Dynasty had completely lost the confidence and respect of its subjects."[86] The remaining kings of the Eighteenth Dynasty—Smenkhkare, Tutankhamun, and Ay—are unable to arrest the decline in Egyptian power and prestige which began after the death of Tuthmosis IV. Only Horemheb, a distinguished general during the reign of Tutankhamun, is able to restore a semblance of Egyptian prestige in the Levant[87] as a result of several campaigns. Horemheb longs for the glory days of the empire and decides that the only way to bring this about is to usurp the throne of Egypt himself. He does just that. So miserable is the Amarna Period in the mind of Horemheb that he marks the beginning of his reign from the death of Amenhotep III, skipping over Akhenaten, Smenkhkare, Tutankhamun and Ay.[88] Before he dies, Horemheb names his fellow general Rameses I to succeed him. Thus ends the once-great Eighteenth Dynasty, and so begins the Nineteenth Dynasty. (yd213-254)

We clearly see from this scenario that the Eighteenth Dynasty can be divided into two distinct periods: (a) from beginning to glory and (b) from decline to demise. The first period, which lasted nearly 160 years, began with the reunification of the kingdom under Amosis after the removal of the Hyksos from Lower Egypt and continued until the empire reached its peak of power and prestige during the reign of Tuthmosis IV. The second period, which lasted about 70 years, began with the erosion of the empire during the reign of Amenhotep III and ended when general Horemheb wrested control of the Egyptian throne, terminating the Eighteenth Dynasty. The fact that Horemheb viewed the last few rulers of the Eighteenth Dynasty—from Akhenaten to Ay—with disgust is, in itself, testimony to the pathetic state of affairs into which Egypt had fallen since the glory days of the empire. Within that period of decline, Egypt suffered several major setbacks:

---

86 Redford, *Egypt, Canaan* 179.
87 Horemheb longed to return to the glory days of the empire, but had to battle with the grim reality that Egypt's former Syrian territories were gone forever. The Nineteenth Dynasty could fare no better.
88 White, *Egypt* 175-176.

- The loss of Syria to the Hittites (late Amenhotep III/early Akhenaten)

- A virtual loss of hegemony in Canaan (late Amenhotep III/early Akhenaten)

- Serious damage to its trans-Euphratian ally, Mittani, at the hands of the Hittites (late Amenhotep III/early Akhenaten)

- The collapse of hegemony in Canaan (early Akhenaten)

- The final collapse of Mittani at the hands of Hatti and Assyria (under Akhenaten).

It is remarkable how, just fifty years after the death of Tuthmosis IV, Egypt was reduced from its dominant position as the Near East's leading superpower to the level of a third-ranking nation nearly imploding upon itself; again, we must ask the question: Why?

What were the Egyptians suffering in such propagandistic silence? When Hatti began to annex Syria—as far south as Lebanon—were the armies of the warrior-king Suppiluliuma really so formidable that the combined strength of Egypt and Mittani could not overcome them? When the Hittites mounted a direct assault on the Mittanian capital, Wassukani, was Egypt's commitment to its "brother" Mittanians really so weak that Suppiluliuma was allowed to crush Mittani without Egypt lifting a finger to defend its long-time ally? When Egyptian vassals in Syria and Canaan cried out to both Amenhotep III and Akhenaten for troops to protect them from the regional turmoil exacerbated by Suppiluliuma, why did those pharaohs turn a deaf ear? Why did the mighty Eighteenth Dynasty—whose very traditions flaunted the idea of a northeastern Euphrates border and an iron-fisted hegemony over Canaanite territories from which it received bounteous tribute of olive oil, wine, and a host of other commodities—suddenly relax its grip on long-held Asiatic provinces, assuming an internal focus that eventually drove the dynasty to extinction? Surely, there is more going on here than meets the eye (see Figures 1 and 2).

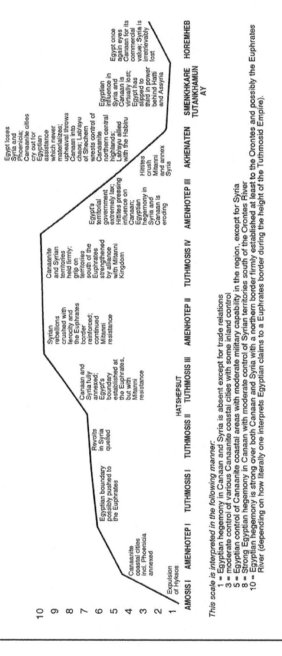

The Relative Strength of Egyptian Hegemony in Canaan and Syria During the 18th Dynasty

This scale is interpreted in the following manner:

1 = Egyptian hegemony in Canaan and Syria is absent except for trade relations
3 = moderate control of various Canaanite coastal cities with some inland control
5 = Egyptian control of Canaanite coastal areas with moderate military capability in the region, except for Syria
8 = Strong Egyptian hegemony in Canaan with moderate control of Syrian territories south of the Orontes River
10 = Egyptian hegemony is strong over both Canaan and Syria with a northern border firmly established at least to the Orontes and possibly the Euphrates River (depending on how literally one interprets Egyptian claims to a Euphrates border during the height of the Tuthmosid Empire).

Figure 1. This linear diagram depicts the relative strength of Egyptian presence/power in Syria and Canaan (= biblical Canaan), and does not suggest the overall strength or wealth of Egypt at any given point in time. However, given the New Kingdom's perennial desire to dominate those Asiatic territories, one cannot but ponder the reasons for hegemonic disintegration and resurgence when they occur.

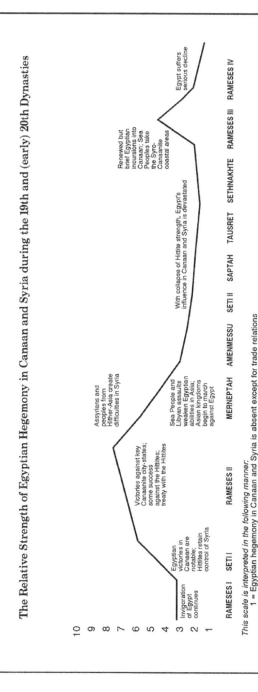

Figure 2. This linear diagram depicts the relative strength of Egyptian presence/power in Syria and Canaan (= biblical Canaan), and does not suggest the overall strength or wealth of Egypt at any given point in time. However, given the New Kingdom's perennial desire to dominate those Asiatic territories, one cannot but ponder the reasons for hegemonic disintegration and resurgence when they occur.

CHAPTER SIX

The Biblical and Egyptian Components Superimposed

—ᴟᴟ—

A s I have discussed previously, if the Exodus scenario presented in the Bible is accepted as historically accurate, then specific predictions about the impact of those events upon Egypt are inevitable.[89] I have also shown that it is reasonable to expect that, in some detectable fashion, the impact of the Exodus core events upon Egypt would likely manifest itself in ancient Near Eastern documents, though likely camouflaged by mythology and propagandistic subjectivism. If this is actually the case, then a side-by-side comparison of the serial history of the Exodus with various segments of Egyptian history should reveal where the Exodus chronology fits best. Obviously, the placement of the Israelite Exodus that produces the greatest number of historical synchronisms, based on predictions arising from the Exodus scenario itself, is most probably the correct one.

SUPERIMPOSITION OF THE BIBLICAL EXODUS SCENARIO UPON A SERIAL HISTORY OF THE EIGHTEENTH DYNASTY

The parallel comparisons that follow are based on several premises, which I have already explained; but allow me to reiterate them briefly:

---

89   Again, I stress the importance of the impact of the Exodus core events on Egypt. If we take the biblical text seriously, then we must expect that, as a result of the Exodus scenario, Egypt would have been significantly affected, possibly requiring a prolonged process of recovery.

1. The literal biblical numbers relative to the Exodus scenario are at least closely rounded approximations. Thus, (a) the Exodus took place about 480 years (440 in the LXX) before the fourth year of Solomon's reign; (b) the 40/40/40 years' configuration of Moses' life is accurate; (c) Jacob stood before Pharaoh about 215 years before the Exodus; (d) the Conquest led by Joshua began about 40 years after the Exodus.

2. Hexateuchal references to Egypt primarily refer to Lower Egypt; i.e., the focal point of Hebrew/Israelite contact with Egypt was the Nile Delta region.

3. From a historiographical point of view, the biblical text is more accurate and objective in what it describes than Egyptian documents.

4. The Pharaoh of the Exodus died in the *yam suph*.

Comparisons will be made using the Briggs Weighted-Average Chronology[90] of Egypt (see Table 2) because of the divergence of scholarly opinion about how the chronology of the Eighteenth Dynasty should be configured. Briggs has provided a good working average of the most accepted chronologies. (Remember that I am not using absolute dating configurations from these chronologies, but elements of relative dating in order to determine the lengths of each reign.) (See Tables 11, 12, and 13 in the Appendix for chronologies other than those of Briggs.) By placing the Exodus at the death of candidate pharaohs, it is possible to ascertain the general correspondence of biblical and Egyptian data for each placement, based on biblical predictions from the Exodus core events.

Rameses II as the Exodus Pharaoh

Even though I will focus mainly on Eighteenth Dynasty pharaohs, I feel that I must apply the historical synchronism method to the reign of Rameses II, if for no other reason than that so many scholars place the Exodus during his reign. For this linear comparison, I have placed the Exodus at three different locations in the (low) chronology of Rameses II: early in the reign of Rameses (see Table 8 and Figure 9 in

---

90   Briggs, *Testing* 39.

the Appendix), in the mid-reign of Rameses (see Table 9 and Figure 10 in the Appendix), and at the death of Rameses (see Table 10 and Figure 11 in the Appendix). Immediately, the lack of correspondence between the Exodus events and the reign of Rameses II becomes obvious.

If we place the Exodus early in Rameses' reign (say, in year 10 of his 66 years of rule), then we must look for some sort of decline in Egyptian power at about that time; but, in fact, there is no evidence of a slump in Egyptian strength during the reign of Rameses. This would also place the beginning of the Conquest during Rameses' reign. Biblically this is a problem because Egyptian hegemony in Canaan was quite strong during most of Rameses' reign,[91] yet the Bible makes it very clear that the Promised Land to be conquered by Joshua was specifically the land of the Canaanites, Amorites, and Hittites, without Egyptian interference. Neither Egyptians nor Egyptian troops are ever encountered by the Israelites anywhere in the book of Joshua. Further, given a 215-year Egyptian sojourn, this placement of the Exodus would put Joseph in Egypt during the height of the Eighteenth Dynasty, which makes little sense given the severe anti-Asiatic (Semitic) sentiments of that period. Thus, those who place the Exodus in the reign of Rameses are always forced to adopt a long (430-year) sojourn in order to get Joseph back into the Hyksos Period, or earlier, where he obviously belongs (see my discussion in Appendix Two).

If the Exodus is placed in the mid-reign of Rameses, then we still have the same problems. However, it is worse because the Conquest would then have begun toward the end of Merneptah's reign, at a time when the Merneptah Stele[92] had already included Israel as one of the 'Nine Bows'—i.e., one of the nine recognized enemies of Egypt—none of which makes any sense at all.

If we place the Exodus at the time of Rameses' death, then relative to historical synchronisms, everything falls apart. That would place the beginning of the Conquest five or six pharaonic generations after Merneptah who had already identified Israel (of central Canaan) as one

---

91   See K.A. Kitchen, *Pharaoh Triumphant: The Life and Times of Ramesses II* (Warminster: Aris and Phillips, 1982).

92   J.B. Pritchard, ed., "Hymn of Victory of Merneptah (The 'Israel Stela')" *ANET*, third ed. (Princeton: Princeton University, 1969) 376-378.

of his perennial enemies. If we take the biblical account of the Exodus seriously, then there are virtually no historical synchronisms visible during the reign of Rameses II.

Another potentially serious problem for late-date theorists comes from the book of Judges, which reports that the Israelite Judge Othniel defeated "Cushan-Rishathaim king of Aram Naharaim" (Judges 3:8-10). C. Billington argues convincingly that Cushan is a ruler of the Mittani Kingdom[93] (see my expanded discussion in Chapter Seven, Point Twenty-seven). If this is so, then Othniel's defeat of Cushan must have occurred prior to the demise of Mittani in the mid- to late-14th century BCE. Indeed, "the story of Othniel's defeat of King Cushan of the Kingdom of Mittani lends very strong support for the Early Date Theory of the Exodus"[94] during the Eighteenth Dynasty.

Candidate Pharaohs from the Eighteenth Dynasty

The literal biblical placement of the Exodus is during the Eighteenth Dynasty in the mid-15th century BCE. But which Egyptian king is most likely the Exodus Pharaoh? We can best identify this most-likely pharaoh by placing the Exodus at the death of several candidates, in order to determine which produces the largest number of historical synchronisms based on the consequences for Egypt predicted by the Exodus core events.

I have removed Tuthmosis IV from his normal position in the following sequence and have placed him last for two reasons. First, before considering him as a candidate for Exodus Pharaoh, I want to look at the Eighteenth Dynasty kings who have already been suggested by various scholars. I find it interesting that although Tuthmosis IV's grandfather, father, son, and grandson have all been considered as the villain of the Exodus story, no one, to my knowledge, has ever suggested him. Second, I want to develop my expanded discussion of historical synchronisms in connection with Tuthmosis IV because, as I hope to demonstrate, placing the Exodus at the end of his reign unlocks a remarkable sequence of synchronisms between the Hexateuchal narratives and Egyptian history.

---

93   C.E. Billington, "Othniel, Cushan-Rishathaim, and the Date of the Exodus," paper presented to the NEAS (2001).
94   Ibid. 11.

Tuthmosis III. If the Exodus occurred about the time of the death of Tuthmosis III (see Table 3 and Figure 3), then Moses was born during the reign of Amenhotep I and his flight from Egypt took place in the reign of Hatshepsut. This also places Joseph in Egypt during the Hyksos Period. Thus, for the pre-Exodus events, there is potential for reasonable correspondence. However, from the point of Tuthmosis' death onward, this placement of the Exodus scenario fails to produce adequate parallels in light of the anticipated impact of the Exodus core events on the Egyptian empire (see Chapter Five, Point Seven). The most glaring failure of this placement of the Exodus is that, upon the death of Tuthmosis III, his son Amenhotep II secured the empire with bold military and administrative activities so that there was absolutely no diminution of Egypt's power and prestige. Amenhotep's hegemony over Canaan and Syria remained strong throughout his reign. There is no indication whatsoever that Egypt experienced a catastrophe of any magnitude in the Delta region before or after the death of Tuthmosis III. If such had occurred, Amenhotep II's ability to successfully control the Asiatic provinces would have suffered.

In addition, this placement fails as the timeframe for the post-Exodus events because the Conquest would then have to be placed very early in the reign of Amenhotep III. Biblically this is problematic because at the outset of his reign Egyptian hegemony in Canaan and Syria, although beginning to slip, was still substantial. Had the Israelite army entered Canaan during the early years of Amenhotep III's reign, they would have encountered an Egyptian military presence, something that the text of Joshua minimizes to the point of omission.

Placing the Exodus at the time of Tuthmosis III's death does not yield the kinds of synchronisms required if we take the biblical Exodus scenario seriously.

Amenhotep II. If the Exodus is moved to correspond with the death of Amenhotep II (see Table 4 and Figure 4), then the context for historical synchronisms improves. With this placement, the plausibility of pre-Exodus synchronisms remains good: Joseph was in Egypt during the time of the Hyksos, and Moses' birth occurred at the beginning of Hatshepsut's reign. Moses' flight from Egypt took place under Tuthmosis

III, and he returned to Egypt to demand that Amenhotep II release the enslaved Israelites. All of this is within the realm of possibility, and it fits well within the context of the Empire Period.

Such a placement of the Exodus puts the Israelite Conquest of Canaan within the final decade of the reign of Amenhotep III. This may be reasonable because, by that time, the disintegration of Egyptian hegemony in Canaan would have been advanced enough to allow Joshua to enter Canaan with little or no Egyptian interference. One glaring problem for an Exodus date corresponding with the death of Amenhotep II is the fact that his son, Tuthmosis IV, thoroughly maintains, and even strengthens, the Egyptian empire through both military might and brilliant diplomacy. Upon and after the death of Amenhotep II, there is absolutely no blip on the historical radar suggesting that anything of negative impact occurred in Lower Egypt. The wealth and power of the Egyptian empire, including a strong hegemony over its Canaanite and Syrian territories, continued unabated through the reign of Tuthmosis IV.[95] Again, the factuality of the biblical Exodus scenario demands the economic and military decimation of the Nile Delta region, and nothing of the sort occurred at the end of Amenhotep II's reign. Thus, although some historical synchronisms seem possible with Amenhotep II as the Exodus Pharaoh, essential correlations are still absent.

Amenhotep III. Less frequently suggested as the Pharaoh of the Exodus than some other candidates, Amenhotep III[96] is, for the purpose of historical synchronisms, a relatively good candidate for that dubious honor. If the Exodus occurred at the end of the reign of Amenhotep III (see Table 5 and Figure 5), then Joseph was in Egypt during the Hyksos Period. Further, Moses was born during the latter part of the reign of Tuthmosis III and fled to Midian from the presence of Tuthmosis IV. All of this works reasonably well.

A potential synchronism for this placement of the Exodus is the fact that even though the empire began to decline during the long reign of Amenhotep III, Egypt's problems worsened dramatically during the reign

---

95   Reeves, *Akhenaten* 51.
96   For a literal understanding of 1 Kings 6:1, the traditional dates for the reign of Amenhotep III
      may just be too late to place the Exodus at the time of his death.

of his son, Akhenaten. It is possible to view the precipitous decline of Egyptian hegemony in Canaan and Syria during Akhenaten's reign as a sign that something had gone so seriously wrong in the Delta region that Egypt was unable to respond to the woeful cries of its vassals for Egyptian military aid in the face of impending destruction. However, this synchronism is weakened by our knowledge of the empire's decline and resultant territorial losses during the reign of Amenhotep III, and by the realization that this decline simply continued under Akhenaten, although at an accelerated pace.

One biblical problem with Amenhotep III as Pharaoh of the Exodus is that it requires the Conquest to begin in the middle of Horemheb's reign, at a time when Egypt had reestablished control over some of its former Canaanite vassals. This means that Joshua would have encountered an Egyptian military and/or administrative presence in Canaan, something that is entirely absent from the biblical record. Further, with Amenhotep III and Akhenaten, whom I will consider next, it is likely that both the Egyptian and biblical chronologies would be stretched too severely to conform to a literal Exodus date.

Akhenaten. If Akhenaten was the pharaoh who died in the *yam suph*, then we can well imagine that, at the very least, the priests of Amun-Re would have stood on the shore and cheered. If the Exodus took place at the end of Akhenaten's reign (see Table 6 and Figure 6), then Joseph would have come to Egypt too late in the Hyksos Period to have finished his viziership before the beginning of the Eighteenth Dynasty. That does not work at all. But Moses' birth during Amenhotep II's reign and his flight from Egypt under Amenhotep III would not be unreasonable. At the death of Akhenaten, Egypt had long been in decline in terms of its former imperial holdings, so that the impact of the Exodus core events would only have exacerbated the problems that already existed.

Beside the fact that the reign of Akhenaten is probably much too late to allow his death to correspond to a literal date for the Exodus, this placement makes the Israelite Conquest of Canaan contemporaneous with the very end of Horemheb's reign. As I have already observed, Horemheb's military background and desire to see Egypt return to the glory days of the empire drove him to launch campaigns into Canaan in order to reestablish Egyptian control there. This does not harmonize well with the book of Joshua which suggests a time when Egypt's presence in Canaan was so diminished, or nonexistent, that it was not even worth mentioning.

The Reigns of the Egyptian Kings of the 18th Dynasty in Regnal and Dynasty Years (Briggs Weighted-Average Chronology[1])

	LENGTH OF REIGN	DYNASTY YEARS
2nd Intermediate Period (Hyksos)	(100 years)	(0-100)
Amosis I	(24 years)	(0-24)
Amenhotep I	(21 years)	(24-45)
Tuthmosis I	(12 years)	(45-57)
Tuthmosis II	(10 years)	(57-67)
Hatshepsut*	(21* years)	(67-88*)
Tuthmosis III	(54 years)	(67-121)
Amenhotep II	(26 years)	(121-147)
Tuthmosis IV	(11 years)	(147-158)
Amenhotep III	(38 years)	(158-196)
Amenhotep IV (Akhenaten)	(17 years)	(196-213)
Smenkhkare**	(2** years)	(211-213**)
Tutankhamun	(9 years)	(213-222)
Ay	(4 years)	(222-226)
Horemheb	(28 years)	(226-254)
18th Dynasty TOTAL	(254 years)	(254 years)

[1] P. Briggs, *Testing the Factuality of the Conquest of Ai Narrative in the Book of Joshua* (doctoral dissertation, Newburgh: Trinity Theological Seminary, 2001) 39.
*co-regency with Tuthmosis III
**co-regency with Akhenaten

Table 2.

**The Reigns of the Egyptian Kings of the 18th Dynasty
in Regnal and Dynasty Years with Select Biblical Events
Using Tuthmosis III as the Pharaoh of the Exodus
(Briggs Weighted-Average Chronology[1])**

	LENGTH OF REIGN	DYNASTY YEARS	BIBLICAL CHRONOLOGY
2nd Intermediate Period (Hyksos)	(100 years)	(0-100)	Joseph in Egypt y_d6 Jacob in Egypt Israelites in Egypt
Amosis I	(24 years)	(0-24)	
Amenhotep I	(21 years)	(24-45)	y_d41 birth of Moses
Tuthmosis I	(12 years)	(45-57)	
Tuthmosis II	(10 years)	(57-67)	
Hatshepsut*	(21* years)	(67-88*)	y_d81 Moses flees Egypt
Tuthmosis III	(54 years)	(67-121)	y_d121 Moses leads Exodus
Amenhotep II	(26 years)	(121-147)	
Tuthmosis IV	(11 years)	(147-158)	
Amenhotep III	(38 years)	(158-196)	y_d161 death of Moses Conquest begins
Amenhotep IV (Akhenaten)	(17 years)	(196-213)	
Smenkhkare**	(2** years)	(211-213**)	
Tutankhamun	(9 years)	(213-222)	
Ay	(4 years)	(222-226)	
Horemheb	(28 years)	(226-254)	
TOTAL	(254 years)	(254 years)	

[1] P. Briggs, *Testing the Factuality of the Conquest of Ai Narrative in the Book of Joshua* (Doctoral Dissertation, Newburgh: Trinity Theological Seminary, 2001) 39.
*co-regency with Tuthmosis III
**co-regency with Akhenaten

Table 3.

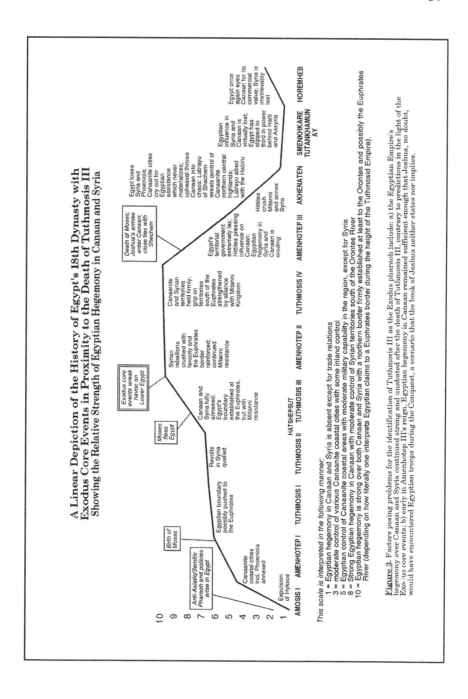

Figure 3. Factors posing problems for the identification of Tuthmosis III as the Exodus pharaoh include: a) the Egyptian Empire's hegemony over Canaan and Syria continued strong and unabated after the death of Tuthmosis III, contrary to predictions in the light of the Exodus core events; b) early in Amenhotep III's reign, Egyptian hegemony in Canaan remained sufficient enough that Joshua, no doubt, would have encountered Egyptian troops during the Conquest, a scenario that the book of Joshua neither states nor implies.

**The Reigns of the Egyptian Kings of the 18th Dynasty
in Regnal and Dynasty Years with Select Biblical Events
Using Amenhotep II as the Pharaoh of the Exodus
(Briggs Weighted-Average Chronology[1])**

	LENGTH OF REIGN	DYNASTY YEARS	BIBLICAL CHRONOLOGY
2nd Intermediate Period (Hyksos)	(100 years)	(0-100)	Joseph in Egypt y_d32 Jacob in Egypt Israelites in Egypt
Amosis I	(24 years)	(0-24)	y_d2 anti-Asiatic Pharaoh and policies arise
Amenhotep I	(21 years)	(24-45)	in Egypt
Tuthmosis I	(12 years)	(45-57)	
Tuthmosis II	(10 years)	(57-67)	
Hatshepsut*	(21* years)	(67-88*)	y_d67 birth of Moses
Tuthmosis III	(54 years)	(67-121)	y_d107 Moses flees Egypt
Amenhotep II	(26 years)	(121-147)	y_d147 Moses leads Exodus
Tuthmosis IV	(11 years)	(147-158)	
Amenhotep III	(38 years)	(158-196)	y_d187 death of Moses Conquest begins
Amenhotep IV (Akhenaten)	(17 years)	(196-213)	
Smenkhkare**	(2** years)	(211-213**)	
Tutankhamun	(9 years)	(213-222)	
Ay	(4 years)	(222-226)	
Horemheb	(28 years)	(226-254)	
18th Dynasty TOTAL	(254 years)	(254 years)	

[1] P. Briggs, *Testing the Factuality of the Conquest of Ai Narrative in the Book of Joshua* (Doctoral Dissertation, Newburgh: Trinity Theological Seminary, 2001) 39.
*co-regency with Tuthmosis III
**co-regency with Akhenaten

Table 4.

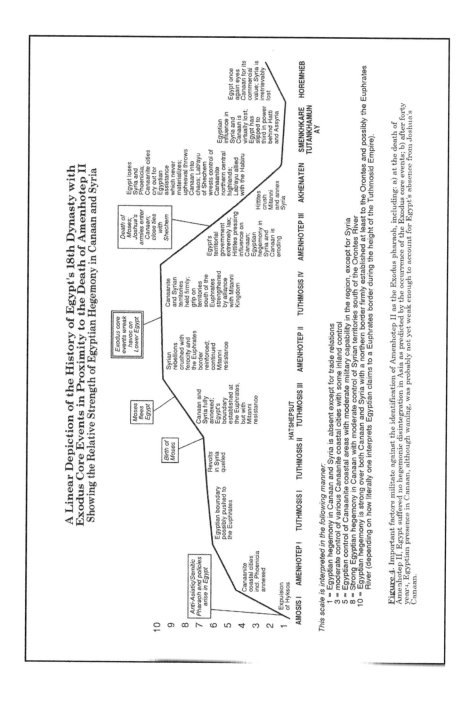

A Linear Depiction of the History of Egypt's 18th Dynasty with Exodus Core Events in Proximity to the Death of Amenhotep II Showing the Relative Strength of Egyptian Hegemony in Canaan and Syria

This scale is interpreted in the following manner:

1 = Egyptian hegemony in Canaan and Syria is absent except for trade relations
3 = moderate control of various Canaanite coastal cities with some inland control
5 = Egyptian control of Canaanite coastal areas with moderate military capability in the region, except for Syria
8 = Strong Egyptian hegemony in Canaan with moderate control of Syrian territories south of the Orontes River
10 = Egyptian hegemony is strong over both Canaan and Syria with a northern border firmly established at least to the Orontes and possibly the Euphrates River (depending on how literally one interprets Egyptian claims to a Euphrates border during the height of the Tuthmosid Empire).

Figure 4. Important factors militate against the identification of Amenhotep II as the Exodus pharaoh, including: a) at the death of Amenhotep II, Egypt suffered no hegemonic disintegration in Asia as predicted by the occurrence of the Exodus core events; b) after forty years, Egyptian presence in Canaan, although waning, was probably not yet weak enough to account for Egypt's absence from Joshua's Canaan.

**The Reigns of the Egyptian Kings of the 18th Dynasty
in Regnal and Dynasty Years with Select Biblical Events
Using Amenhotep III as the Pharaoh of the Exodus
(Briggs Weighted-Average Chronology[1])**

	LENGTH OF REIGN	DYNASTY YEARS	BIBLICAL CHRONOLOGY
2nd Intermediate Period (Hyksos)	(100 years)	(0-100)	Joseph in Egypt y_d81 Jacob in Egypt Israelites in Egypt
Amosis I	(24 years)	(0-24)	
Amenhotep I	(21 years)	(24-45)	
Tuthmosis I	(12 years)	(45-57)	y_d51 anti-Asiatic Pharaoh and policies arise in Egypt
Tuthmosis II	(10 years)	(57-67)	
Hatshepsut*	(21* years)	(67-88*)	
Tuthmosis III	(54 years)	(67-121)	y_d116 birth of Moses
Amenhotep II	(26 years)	(121-147)	
Tuthmosis IV	(11 years)	(147-158)	y_d156 Moses flees Egypt
Amenhotep III	(38 years)	(158-196)	y_d196 Moses leads Exodus
Amenhotep IV (Akhenaten)	(17 years)	(196-213)	
Smenkhkare**	(2** years)	(211-213**)	
Tutankhamun	(9 years)	(213-222)	
Ay	(4 years)	(222-226)	
Horemheb	(28 years)	(226-254)	y_d236 death of Moses Conquest begins
18th Dynasty TOTAL	(254 years)	(254 years)	

[1] P. Briggs, *Testing the Factuality of the Conquest of Ai Narrative in the Book of Joshua* (Doctoral Dissertation, Newburgh: Trinity Theological Seminary, 2001) 39.
*co-regency with Tuthmosis III
**co-regency with Akhenaten

Table 5.

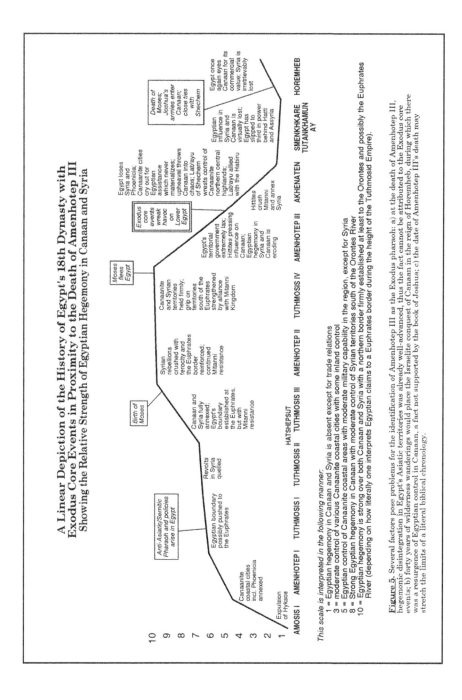

Figure 5. Several factors pose problems for the identification of Amenhotep III as the Exodus pharaoh: a) at the death of Amenhotep III, hegemonic disintegration in Egypt's Asiatic territories was already well-advanced, thus the fact cannot be attributed to the Exodus core events; b) forty years of wilderness wanderings would place the Israelite conquest of Canaan in the reign of Horemheb, during which there was a resurgence of Egyptian control in Canaan, a fact not supported by the book of Joshua; c) the date of Amenhotep III's death may stretch the limits of a literal biblical chronology.

The Reigns of the Egyptian Kings of the 18th Dynasty in Regnal and Dynasty Years with Select Biblical Events Using Akhenaten as the Pharaoh of the Exodus (Briggs Weighted-Average Chronology[1])

	LENGTH OF REIGN	DYNASTY YEARS	BIBLICAL CHRONOLOGY
2nd Intermediate Period (Hyksos)	(100 years)	(0-100)	Joseph in Egypt y₄98 Jacob in Egypt Israelites in Egypt
Amosis I	(24 years)	(0-24)	
Amenhotep I	(21 years)	(24-45)	
Tuthmosis I	(12 years)	(45-57)	
Tuthmosis II	(10 years)	(57-67)	
Hatshepsut*	(21* years)	(67-88*)	
Tuthmosis III	(54 years)	(67-121)	anti-Asiatic Pharaoh y₄68 and policies arise in Egypt
Amenhotep II	(26 years)	(121-147)	y₄133 birth of Moses
Tuthmosis IV	(11 years)	(147-158)	
Amenhotep III	(38 years)	(158-196)	y₄173 Moses flees Egypt
Amenhotep IV (Akhenaten)	(17 years)	(196-213)	y₄213 Moses leads Exodus
Smenkhkare**	(2** years)	(211-213**)	
Tutankhamun	(9 years)	(213-222)	
Ay	(4 years)	(222-226)	
Horemheb	(28 years)	(226-254)	y₄253 death of Moses Conquest begins
18th Dynasty TOTAL	(254 years)	(254 years)	

[1] P. Briggs, *Testing the Factuality of the Conquest of Ai Narrative in the Book of Joshua* (Doctoral Dissertation, Newburgh: Trinity Theological Seminary, 2001) 39.
*co-regency with Tuthmosis III
**co-regency with Akhenaten

Table 6.

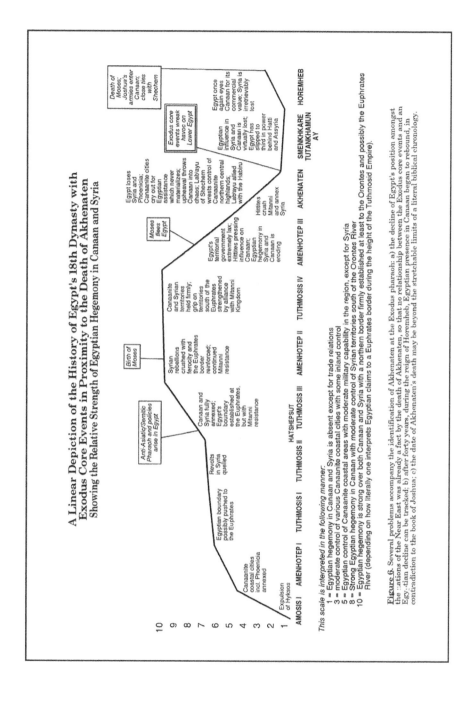

A Linear Depiction of the History of Egypt's 18th Dynasty with Exodus Core Events in Proximity to the Death of Akhenaten Showing the Relative Strength of Egyptian Hegemony in Canaan and Syria

This scale is interpreted in the following manner:

1 = Egyptian hegemony in Canaan and Syria is absent except for trade relations
3 = moderate control of various Canaanite coastal cities with some inland control
5 = Egyptian control of Canaanite coastal areas with moderate military capability in the region, except for Syria
8 = Strong Egyptian hegemony in Canaan with moderate control of Syrian territories south of the Orontes River
10 = Egyptian hegemony is strong over both Canaan and Syria with a northern border firmly established at least to the Orontes and possibly the Euphrates River (depending on how literally one interprets Egyptian claims to a Euphrates border during the height of the Tuthmosid Empire).

Figure 6. Several problems accompany the identification of Akhenaten at the Exodus pharaoh: a) the decline of Egypt's position amongst the nations of the Near East was already a fact by the death of Akhenaten, so that no relationship between the Exodus core events and an Egyptian decline can be tracked; b) after forty years, during the reign of Horemheb, Egyptian presence in Canaan began to rebound, in contradiction to the book of Joshua; c) the date of Akhenaten's death may be beyond the stretchable limits of a literal biblical chronology.

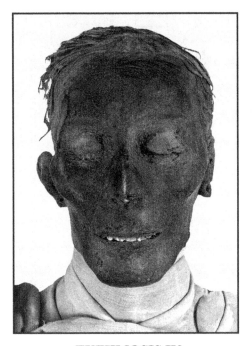

TUTHMOSIS IV

CHAPTER SEVEN

Pharoah of the Exodus: Tuthmosis IV

—〰—

If Tuthmosis IV was the Pharaoh of the Exodus (see Table 7 and Figure 7), then the combined impact of the core events of the Exodus scenario (see Chapter Four)—the ten plagues, the plundering of wealth, the loss of a large labor force, the loss of Delta military forces, and the death of Pharaoh—would have had an immediate effect on the ability of the Egyptian empire, then arguably at its peak, to maintain a grip on its Asiatic territories. (See Tables 14, 15 and 16 in the Appendix for other chronologies using Tuthmosis IV as the Exodus Pharaoh.)

That is precisely what happened upon the death of Tuthmosis IV (see Chapter Five, Point Eleven). In fact, at no other point in the history of the Eighteenth Dynasty can any clearer line of demarcation be drawn between imperial strength and the beginning of Egypt's decline. At the point of Tuthmosis IV's death, what is predicted of Egypt on the basis of the Exodus core events actually took place. In the reign of his son, Amenhotep III, a definite decline in Egyptian hegemony over Canaan and Syria ensued. During the transition years from Amenhotep III to Amenhotep IV, the Hittites, with impunity, attacked Mittani and took control of Syria. By the early reign of Amenhotep IV, Egypt had, for all practical purposes, lost control of its Asiatic territories and was experiencing a decline, particularly in terms of its former imperial vision.

With Tuthmosis IV as Pharaoh of the Exodus, historical synchronisms align most realistically. The best way to demonstrate them is to present, side-by-side, the 27 points of the serial summary of the Exodus events, commenting on each synchronism as it relates to the Egyptian historical progression, using "biblical years" (=yb with Exodus at yb0) and "dynasty years" (=yd with Exodus at yd158, the death of Tuthmosis IV). I will also note those elements of cultural specificity that are relevant to the historical authenticity of the biblical narrative.

Point One: Joseph is sold to Midianite caravaners and taken to Egypt where he becomes a slave. (yb-230; yd-72) (Gen 37ff) Slavery became an institution in Egypt during the Middle Kingdom, and the Hyksos of the Second Intermediate Period, who were rigorous about things Egyptian, surely followed suit. We should also note that the payment for Joseph was twenty shekels of silver, the going price of a slave in the Middle Bronze Age.[97]

Point Two: Joseph becomes vizier of Egypt, second administratively only to Pharaoh himself, and is introduced to the populace via a chariot processional. (yb-226; yd-68) (Genesis 41:37ff) That Joseph, an Asiatic Semite, could have been elevated to vizier under the rule of the Semitic Hyksos is entirely reasonable. Also, most scholars agree that the Hyksos introduced the chariot into Egypt,[98] making that period an ideal setting for the story of Joseph.

Point Three: Due to conditions of famine in Canaan, Jacob and the Israelite tribes move to reside in Lower Egypt. (yb-217; yd-59) (Genesis 47:9ff) The latter part of the Middle Bronze Age in Canaan was marked by considerable unrest and resultant population movements. Numerous factors, including possible famine, drove Asiatics into the Nile Delta region, including those later known to us as the Hyksos. Although the population of Canaan had burgeoned during the MBA, it decreased in the LBA possibly due in part to

---

97   Kitchen, "Patriarchal Age" 52.
98   A.R. Schulman, "Chariots, Chariotry and the Hyksos," *JSSEA* 10 (1980) 105-153. See also P.R.S. Moorey, "The Emergence of the Light, Horse-Drawn Chariot in the Near East c. 2000-1500 B.C.," *WA* 18.2 (1986), 196-215; and J.H. Crouwel and M.A. Littauer, "Chariots," *OEANE* Vol. 1 (New York and Oxford: Oxford University Press, 1997) 485-487.

climatological changes.[99] It is also interesting that recent discoveries of Proto-Sinaitic inscriptions in Upper Egypt confirm the invention of that early alphabet by Semitic peoples living in Egypt during the Second Intermediate Period[100]—an alphabet that would later find its way into the Sinai region during the 15th century BCE,[101] about the time of the Exodus.

Point Four: Jacob stands before Pharaoh; the Israelite sojourn in Lower Egypt begins (see Appendix Two). (yb-215; yd-57) (Genesis 47:7ff; Exodus 1:1ff) The Hyksos retained, no doubt, their ability to speak their native Canaanite tongue, though they usually appear quite Egyptianized in the scant and uncertain records they have left to us. Thus the possibility of face-to-face conversations between the Hebrews and the Hyksos is reasonable.

Point Five: Joseph retires from his Egyptian viziership to live out his life with his people in Lower Egypt. (yb-208; yd-50) (Genesis 47:27ff; by inference) The Hyksos realm was an ideal time and place for a Hebrew (= Asiatic Semitic) family to prosper, especially the family of a retired, but still beloved, vizier.

Point Six: Jacob dies and his funereal event in Canaan is attended by a large company of Egyptian officials. (yb-198; yd-40) (Genesis 49:33-50:9) Such a funeral procession back to the land of Canaan would not have been unusual under the Hyksos domination.

Point Seven: Joseph dies and is given an Egyptian-style burial. (yb-147; yd11) (Genesis 50:26; Exodus 1:6) The Hyksos followed Egyptian practices and traditions with rigor, so the Israelites may

---

99   J.K. Hoffmeier, *Israel in Egypt: The Evidence for the Authenticity of the Exodus Tradition* (New York/Oxford: Oxford U., 1996) 52-76. See also M. Broshi and R. Gophna, "Middle Bronze Age II Palestine: Its Settlements and Population," *BASOR* 261 (1986) 73-90; Aharoni, *Land* 147-176; and I. Finkelstein, "From Sherds to History," *IEJ* 48 (1998) 120-131 (based on a 1996 *Eretz Israel* article by Finkelstein published in Hebrew as "The Settlement History of the Transjordan Plateau in the Light of Survey Data").

100   J.C. Darnell and D. Darnell, "1994-95 Annual Report," *The Luxor-Farshut Desert Road Project* (Chicago: Oriental Institute, University of Chicago, 1997).

101   J. Naveh, *Early History of the Alphabet*, second rev. ed. (Jerusalem: Magnes, 1987) 23-28. Of particular interest is M.A. Oaukin, *Mysteries of the Alphabet* (New York: Abbeyville Press, 1999) 38-111.

have followed Egyptian burial customs in the case of Joseph. Even if Joseph's death occurred during the first part of Amosis' new Eighteenth Dynasty, the burial practices would have been similar.

Point Eight: The sons of Israel begin to multiply greatly. (yb-145; yd13) (Exodus 1:7) The expansion of the Asiatic Semitic population in the Nile Delta region during the opening years of the Eighteenth Dynasty is entirely reasonable.

Point Nine: A king arises in Egypt who "does not know Joseph." (yb-145; yd13) (Exodus 1:8) Amosis is a perfect candidate for this pharaoh.[102] His hatred of the Hyksos forged the subsequent Eighteenth Dynasty policy of suppression and eventual enslavement of Asiatics (see Chapter Five, Point Two).

Point Ten: The Egyptians apply a policy of hatred and persecution against a burgeoning Semitic population in the eastern Nile Delta region of Goshen (Lower Egypt). (yb-145; yd13) (Exodus 1:9ff) This is exactly what happened in Lower Egypt during the reigns of all the early Eighteenth Dynasty kings (see Chapter Five).

Point Eleven: The Hebrews are conscripted, possibly enslaved, in order to build store-cities (the names of which were perhaps later contemporized as Pithom and Rameses) for Pharaoh. (after yb-145; yd13) (Exodus 1:11) Great building projects were launched in Lower Egypt by most of the early Eighteenth and mid-Eighteenth Dynasty pharaohs. So many slaves were needed during the Empire Period that the Egyptians continuously raided Canaan, particularly the central hill country, to capture Asiatics for that purpose. Egypt virtually de-populated parts of Canaan during this time.[103]

Point Twelve: In spite of their difficult servitude, the sons of Israel continue to multiply, to the extent that the Egyptians are "in dread" of them. (yb-85; yd73) (Exodus 1:12) It is logical that Hatshepsut—

---

102 See Hoffmeier, *Israel in Egypt* 122-126. Hoffmeier suggests the rise of Amosis and the expulsion of the Hyksos from Lower Egypt as one of two "plausible scenarios" in the New Kingdom for the "Pharaoh who knew not Joseph."

103 Bryan, "The Eighteenth Dynasty"; see also Hoffmeier, *Israel in Egypt* 109-134, and Hayes, "Tuthmosis I to Amenophis III."

or any other empire pharaoh, for that matter—would have feared a repeat of the infamous Hyksos takeover of Lower Egypt and would have taken the steps necessary to prevent any recurrence of the old "Asiatic problem." [104]

Point Thirteen: The king of Egypt gives orders to kill the male Hebrew infants as a means of population control. (yb-85; yd73) (Exodus 1:15ff) It is not impossible that the Egyptians of the Empire Period would have instituted such drastic measures in order to prevent a repeat of the Hyksos debacle.

Point Fourteen: Moses is born. (yb-80; yd78) (Exodus 2:1ff) Moses' name is obviously not Semitic in origin.[105] In fact, its linguistic equivalency to the "-mosis" component of names (like Amosis and Tuthmosis) common in the Eighteenth Dynasty is unmistakable.[106]

Point Fifteen: Moses flees Egypt into Midianite territory. (yb-40; yd118) (Exodus 2:11ff) This event could have taken place at any time during the New Kingdom.

Point Sixteen: A king of Egypt dies while Moses is in Midian. (yb-10; yd148) (Exodus 2:23) Given that the duration of Moses' exile in Midian was approximately forty years, virtually every placement of the Exodus events in the Eighteenth Dynasty allows the death of at least one pharaoh while Moses is in Midian.

Point Seventeen: Under Yahweh's direction, Moses returns to the court of Pharaoh to demand the release of the Israelites from bondage. (yb-1; yd157) (Exodus 5:1ff) As Yahweh's representative, Moses confronted the most powerful ruler in the Near East. It is reasonable to imagine that only an event, or series of events, that posed a real threat to the continuation of the empire could have successfully led to the final freedom attained by the Israelite tribes.

---

104 Ibid.
105 J.K. Hoffmeier, "Moses," *ISBE*, G.W. Bromiley, gen. ed. (Grand Rapids: Eerdmans, 1986) 417. See also Hoffmeier, *Israel in Egypt* 135-163.
106 Ibid. See also Redford, *Egypt, Canaan* 417-418; Hoerth, *Archaeology* 158; and R. Smend, "Mose als geshichtliche Gestalt," *HZ* 260 (1995) 1-19.

Point Eighteen: Ten successive plagues wreak havoc on Lower Egypt. (yb-1; yd157) (Exodus 7:14-12:34) The implications of these events have been discussed above (see Chapter Four, Point Eighteen). Is it merely coincidence that Tuthmosis IV, at the moment of his untimely death, was an "extremely emaciated man" as reported by G.E. Smith? (see Chapter Five, Point Ten). The impact of the ten plagues could very well have caused Pharaoh to suffer emotionally to the point of pining away.

Point Nineteen: The Hebrews plunder Lower Egypt. (yb-1; yd157) (Exodus 12:35-36) The impact of such an event on Egypt was discussed above (see Chapter Four, Point Nineteen).

Point Twenty: Moses leads the Hebrew tribes and a host of other associated tribes (probably also Semitic) eastward out of Lower Egypt. (yb0; yd158) (Exodus 12:37ff) The negative impact of this event on Egypt was discussed above (see Chapter Four, Point Twenty).

Point Twenty-one: The Israelites camp between "Migdol and the sea." (yb0; yd158) (Exodus 14:2) After the expulsion of the Hyksos from Lower Egypt, the Egyptians built a series of fortifications and garrisons along the bitter lakes region from the Gulf of Suez to the Mediterranean in order to prevent further unwanted incursions of Asiatics from the northeast.[107]

Point Twenty-two: The charioteer Pharaoh leads a sizable Nile Delta-based military force in pursuit of the sons of Israel. (yb0; yd158) (Exodus 14:5ff) Tuthmosis IV is pictured on many of his monuments as a great charioteer "whose horses were fleeter than the wind."[108]

Point Twenty-three: The Egyptian forces, including Pharaoh himself, are drowned in the *yam suph.* (yb0; yd158) (Exodus 14:26ff) The devastating impact of this event on Egypt was discussed above (see Chapter Four, Point Twenty-three).

---

107   See I. Shaw and P. Nicholson, "Borders, Frontiers and Limits," *DAE* (London: British Museum, 1995) 55-56.
108   M.A. Murray, *The Splendor that Was Egypt* (New York: Praeger, 1969) 36-37.

Point Twenty-four: The bodies of the drowned Egyptians are recoverable from the shoreline of the *yam suph*. (yb0; yd158) (Exodus 14:30) The fact that we have the mummy of Tuthmosis IV does not contradict the assumption that Pharaoh died with his troops. According to the Bible, his body would have been recoverable from the shore of the *yam suph*. Egyptian religion demanded the proper burial of the pharaoh.[109]

Point Twenty-five: The Hebrew multitude, led by Moses, travels to Mt. Sinai to receive the laws of Yahweh; as a result of the subsequent Kadesh-Barnea episode, they are directed by Yahweh to live as nomads in the wilderness for the next 38 years. (yb0; yd158) (Exodus 15:1ff; Numbers 13:1ff; Deuteronomy 2:14)

An interesting fact to note at this point is the length of the reign of Amenhotep III. If Tuthmosis IV was the Pharaoh of the Exodus, then the deterioration of the empire as a result of Exodus-related losses in Lower Egypt would have begun during the reign of Amenhotep III; that is precisely what happened. It then took almost the entire reign of Amenhotep for Egypt to lose its grip on Canaan and Syria (= the biblical Promised Land). Was it mere coincidence that the Israelite wilderness wanderings lasted 38 years (Deuteronomy 2:14), precisely the length of the reign of Amenhotep III, after which the Israelite Conquest occurred during the reign of Akhenaten when Egypt had neither the power nor the will to dominate Asian territories? Under this placement of the Exodus, Joshua entered Canaan during a time when Egypt had virtually turned its back on the region.

There are other interesting elements of this timeframe for the Exodus. Although there is certainly no consensus on the location of Mt. Sinai, the Bible implies that it had been used as a worship (cult) center long before Moses discovered it. A site called Har Karkom in northern Sinai with its thousands of examples of ancient graf

---

109 See C. Traunecker, *The Gods of Egypt* (Ithaca and London: Cornell University, 2001); and A.R. David, *The Ancient Egyptians: Religious Beliefs and Practices* (New York and London: Routledge and Kegan Paul, 1982). See also Brier, *Egyptian Mummies*.

fiti—fits this description precisely.[110] I am not suggesting that Har Karkom is necessarily Mt. Sinai, but it demonstrates the reality of such sites in the Sinai prior to the time of Moses. I also think that the presence of Proto-Sinaitic inscriptions in the Sinai during the 15th century BCE (the time of the Exodus), after such writing had been invented in Egypt during the latter part of the MBA (the time of the arrival of the Hebrew patriarchs in Egypt), is more than coincidental.[111]

Additional points of cultural specificity are also worth noting. The Mosaic law code is constructed according to LBA covenant and treaty patterns (not according to later patterns, which are significantly different).[112] In the Mosaic Law, the price of a slave is thirty shekels (Exodus 21:32), which is exactly the average slave price in the early LBA (in later periods the price of slaves is dramatically inflated; for example, the price of a slave in the Persian Period is about 120 shekels.).[113] The report of the Israelite spies at Kadesh-barnea tells of Canaanite cities that "are fortified and very large" (Num 13:28; see also Deut 3:5), which is precisely the nature of cities throughout Canaan during the LBA, particularly those attacked by Joshua during the Conquest (even though some scholars continue to promote the erroneous idea that most LBA cities mentioned in the book of Joshua were not fortified).[114]

Point Twenty-six: Moses dies. (yb40; yd198) (Deuteronomy 34:7) Of course, this fits any placement scenario.

Point Twenty-seven: The Conquest of Canaan by Joshua and the Israelites begins. (yb40; yd198) (Joshua 1ff) With the Exodus tied to the death of Tuthmosis IV, the Israelite Conquest of Canaan would have begun early in the reign of Akhenaten. If that is true, then it is unlikely that Joshua would have encountered any Egyptian resistance, as the Bible suggests he did not. The Amarna Letters not only

110 See A. Anati, *Har Karkom: The Mountain of God* (New York: Rizzoli, 1986).
111 Naveh, *Alphabet* 23-28. See also Darnell and Darnell, "1994-95 Report."
112 Kitchen, "Patriarchal Age" 52-56.
113 Ibid. 52.
114 D.G. Hansen, *Evidence for Fortifications at Late Bronze I and IIA Locations in Palestine* (doctoral dissertation, Newburgh: Trinity Theological Seminary, 2000) provides an excellent treatment of this subject.

testify to the tumultuous nature of the situation in Canaan and Syria at the time, but also to Akhenaten's inability to provide an Egyptian military response to alleviate the situation. Herzog and Gichon assess and describe the state of affairs perfectly:

> Joshua also had to reckon with the prospect of interference by the Egyptians, as Canaan was still part of the Pharaonic empire. We now know from the archives of King Amenhotep IV (Ikhnaton...)...discovered at Tell el-Amarna on the Nile, that most calls for aid from the Canaanites and Egyptian officials alike had been put off with empty promises. And Joshua, though certainly not privy to the Egyptian diplomatic correspondence, did gauge the actual situation correctly. The time was ripe for a strike, and there was little danger of Egyptian interference as long as the Israelites kept to the mountains and away from the plains, the site of the Via Maris (Way of the Sea), the great trade route that connected Egypt with Syria and thus the strategic lifeline of the Egyptian empire.[115]

In the Amarna Letters, it is revealed that the king of the Shechem city-state, Lab'ayu, was accused by other regional city-state rulers of aligning himself with the Habiru, and Lab'ayu's sons were accused of the same offense.[116] Evidently, the Habiru had encamped around Shechem

---

115 C. Herzog and M. Gichon, *Battles of the Bible* (London: Greenhill Books, 2002) 49. See also W.L. Moran, *The Amarna Letters* (Baltimore: Johns Hopkins University, 1992). Interpretations of the Amarna Letters with a view to understanding the socio-political situation in Canaan and Syria during the reigns of Amenhotep III and Akhenaten vary widely. Many scholars think they reflect "business as usual" for the Eighteenth Dynasty, even though we (accidentally?) have no such documents from the reigns of other Eighteenth Dynasty pharaohs. I have concluded that this viewpoint is untenable for several reasons: (a) Eighteenth Dynasty hegemony in Asia definitely erodes during the reigns of Amenhotep III and Akhenaten; (b) neither Amenhotep III nor Akhenaten launch any military action into Canaan or Syria; (c) the Amarna Letters do describe a tumultuous situation in Canaan and Syria; (d) the Hittites attack Egypt's closest ally, Mittani, with impunity; (e) the Hittites, as if they know that Egypt (for the first time in over one hundred years) cannot act to protect its northern interests, take Syria as far south as the mountains of Lebanon; (f) the Dynasty continues to deteriorate until it comes to an end shortly after the reign of Akhenaten; (g) Horemheb views the Amarna Period as an embarrassing episode and seeks to erase it from memory. In my opinion, all this (and there is more) adds up to the fact that Egypt, under the watches of both Amenhotep III and Akhenaten for reasons that remain invisible in its own records, was prevented by internal difficulties from responding to the deteriorating situation in the Levant. Thus, the Amarna pharaohs were not experiencing anything remotely resembling "business as usual." Indeed, any international prestige that Amenhotep III and Akhenaten possessed during their reigns was inherited from the mighty empire left to them by Tuthmosis III, Amenhotep II, and Tuthmosis IV.

116 Moran, *Amarna Letters*; particularly: EA 237, EA 244, EA 245, EA 246, EA 249, EA 250, EA 252, EA 253, EA 254, EA 255, EA 263, EA 280, EA 287, and EA 289. See also Waterhouse, "Habiru" 37-39.

in great numbers and were, indeed, on friendly terms with Lab'ayu and his family. This was all happening early in Akhenaten's reign, and the timing is interesting. With Tuthmosis IV as the Pharaoh of the Exodus, Joshua could have launched the Conquest of Canaan while Lab'ayu was king of Shechem.[117] And by what other term would Canaanite city-dwellers have referred to Joshua's Israelites, since they had all grown up as nomads in the wilderness and would have been perceived as nothing more or less than the marauding rabble they called "Habiru"? Although many scholars have disallowed—on quite flimsy grounds, I think—a relationship between the terms "Habiru" and "Hebrew," there is no doubt about the linguistic similarity of the two terms.[118] It is also worth noting that, according to the biblical text, the Israelites never attacked Shechem or any town belonging to the Shechem city-state. And might not the Akkadian name, Lab'ayu—which in Hebrew is Leba'-Ya = lion of Yahweh—suggest that the king of Shechem was, in some fashion, a worshipper of Yahweh, the God of Joshua (Heb. Yehosua' = Yahweh saves), revealing a possible religious affinity between the two leaders? Although written from radically different points of view, the biblical story of Joshua's association with Shechem as well as the Canaanite perception of Habiru ties to Lab'ayu's Shechem coalition as reflected in the Amarna correspondence seem to me far more than coincidental.

Then there is the matter of Akhenaten's religious reforms. With this placement of the Exodus—at the death of Tuthmosis IV—is it possible

---

117 See Moran, *Amarna Letters* xxxiv-xxxix. A possible co-regency of up to ten years between Amenhotep III and Akhenaten makes the placement of Lab'ayu difficult to determine. An Egyptian "docket" notation on Lab'ayu tablet EA 254 could read either "year 12" or "year 32." As Moran points out, if the correct reading is "year 12," then the reign of Akhenaten is meant; if "year 32" is read, then the late-reign of Amenhotep III is in view. And if the first ten years (or so) of Akhenaten's reign was shared with his father (which is a distinct possibility), then, either way, Akhenaten would have been on the throne during the timeframe of the Lab'ayu correspondence. If the reading of the hieratic docket of EA 254 is uncertain or inaccurate (even "year 2" and "year 22" are possibilities), or if they were somehow mislabeled by an ancient archivist, then all renderings may be incorrect. At any rate, the exact chronology of Lab'ayu remains fuzzy. See F.J. Giles, *The Amarna Age: Western Asia, ACES 5* (Warminster: Aris and Phillips, 1997).
118 Hoerth, *Archaeology* 216-219. It is interesting to note that K.A. Kitchen, although minimizing any linguistic connection between the Apiru (Egyptian equivalent of Akkadian Habiru, meaning "displaced people") and the biblical Hebrews, readily admits that "there are clear behavioral analogies between these Apiru and the displaced Hebrews who had fled Egypt and (now rootless) sought to establish themselves in Canaan." He then proceeds to point out several analogous activities and characteristics between the Habiru/Apiru of the Amarna Letters and the Hebrews led by Joshua. Kitchen also seems to find many parallels between the book of Joshua (and even Exodus) and the historical context of Egypt's Eighteenth Dynasty, even though he personally opts for an Exodus during the reign of Rameses II of the Nineteenth Dynasty! See Kitchen, *Reliability of the Old Testament* 165, 159-312.

to view Akhenaten's quasi-monotheism (Atenism[119]) as a reaction against the gods of Egypt who, during the reign of his grandfather, were powerless to prevent the ten plagues and subsequent Exodus events wrought by the Israelite God, Yahweh? Could the resultant decline of the Egyptian empire under his father, Amenhotep III, have further reinforced Akhenaten's notion that the defeated gods of Egypt were too anemic to preserve the kingdom, and that a new, most-high god, Aten (the sun disc), might help to reinvigorate Egypt? Whatever his motivations for such severe religious reforms, Akhenaten was not able to inhibit Egypt's decline.

Culturally specific elements of the biblical Exodus/Conquest scenario tend to confirm the historical authenticity of its stories and their setting in the Late Bronze Age. For example, listings of cities in the books of Numbers and Joshua, through which the Israelites are said to have traveled, are confirmed by Egyptian "map lists" from New Kingdom pharaohs, such as Tuthmosis III, Amenhotep III, and Rameses II. These Egyptian lists clearly refute the claims of some scholars that certain biblical cities, such as Dibon in Numbers 33 and Hebron in Joshua 15, did not exist in the Late Bronze Age.[120] Further, the known cultural/ linguistic composition of Canaan during the Late Bronze Age is exactly what the Bible describes at the time of Joshua (Num 13:29): Amalekites in the Negev; Hittites, Jebusites and Amorites in the hill country; and Canaanites along the Mediterranean Sea and along the Jordan.[121] A 15th century BCE placement of the Exodus also corresponds to the time and nature of the destruction of both Jericho[122] (Joshua 6) and Ai[123] (Joshua 7-8) toward the end of the LB I or beginning of LB II.

---

119 Traunecker, *Gods* 76, 90-91; David, *Religious Beliefs*.

120 C.R. Krahmalkov, "Exodus Itinerary Confirmed by Egyptian Evidence," *BAR* 20.5 (1994) 55-62.

121 See A.R. Millard, "The Canaanites," M. Liverani, "The Amorites," and H.A. Hoffner, "The Hittites and Hurrians," *Peoples of Old Testament Times*, D.J. Wiseman, ed. (London: Oxford University, 1973) 29-52, 100-133, 197-228. See also H.A. Hoffner, "The Hittites," and K.N. Schoville, "Canaanites and Amorites," *Peoples of the Old Testament World*, Hoerth, Mattingly, and Yamauchi, eds. (Grand Rapids: Baker, 1994) 127-182.

122 B.G. Wood, "Did the Israelites Conquer Jericho?," *BAR* 16.2 (1990) 44-58. See also B.G. Wood, "The Walls of Jericho," *BS* 12.2 (1999) 35-42.

123 B.G. Wood, "Khirbet el-Maqatir, 1995-1998," *IEJ* 50.1-2 (2000) 123-130. See also B.G. Wood, "Khirbet el-Maqatir, 1999," *IEJ* 50.3-4 (2000) 249-254; B.G. Wood, "Khirbet el-Maqatir, 2000," *IEJ* 51.2 (2001) 246-252; B.G. Wood, "Kh. el-Maqatir 2000 Dig Report," *BS* 13.3 (2000) 67-72; and Briggs, *Testing*. Briggs' work is a rigorous scientific application of true narrative representation (TNR) theory (developed by J.W. Oller, Jr.) to the site of Kh. el-Maqatir. He concludes that Kh. el-Maqatir is the most reasonable candidate for biblical Ai. I served for six seasons (1995-2000) as a field supervisor at the Kh. el-Maqatir excavation (under the direction of B.G. Wood) and concur with Briggs' conclusions about the site.

With Tuthmosis IV as the Pharaoh of the Exodus, a most remarkable historical synchronism arises from the book of Judges. This particular synchronism links the mention of a Mittani king in Judges 3:7-11 to a brief window of time toward the end of the Amarna Period. With the Exodus occurring proximate to the death of Tuthmosis IV, there are three keys to this synchronism: (a) the identification of Cushan-Rishathaim, king of Aram-Naharaim as a Mittani ruler; (b) the demise and virtual non-existence of the Mittani Kingdom toward the end of the 14th century BCE; and (c) the death of the well-known Mittani king Tushratta shortly after the end of Akhenaten's reign.

As for the first point, C. Billington has successfully argued that the Cushan of Judges 3:7-11 is a Mittani king on the basis of both geographical and linguistic evidence.[124] There can be little doubt that the name Cushan is not Semitic but of Indo-European origin, as was the Mittani ruling class. Further, the term Rishathaim is directly related to Reshet/Reshu (in Egyptian texts), Rishim/Rish/Urshu (in Ugaritic texts), Urshu (in Eblaite texts), and Urshu (in Hittite texts), and refers to locations in the area of northern Mesopotamia, the region controlled by the Mittani Kingdom during its existence.[125] Billington also demonstrates that the fair-haired Indo-European (Indo-Aryan) Rsi people who invaded India from the north were most likely the same group who came from the north to become the ruling class of the Mittani Kingdom. The link is further solidified by the fact that the Mittani kings invoked gods with Vedic names—Mitra, Varuna, Indra and Nasatyas.[126] I should also point out that the biblical term Naharaim (= between the rivers) is obviously equivalent to the Egyptian term for Mittani, Naharin (or Nakh(ri)ma' as it appears in EA 75 of the Amarna Correspondence[127]).

On the second point, the final destruction of the Mittani Kingdom by the Hittite warrior-king Suppiluliuma toward the end of Akhenaten's reign, and for some time thereafter, sets a *terminus ad quem* for military action into Canaan (or anywhere for that matter) by a Mittani ruler. Once Tushratta had fled his capital, Wassukani, and was subsequently

---

124 See Billington, "Othniel."
125 Ibid. 2-3.
126 Ibid. 3-4.
127 Moran, *Amarna* 145.

murdered, the Kingdom of Mittani lasted only a few more years, of which we know very little.[128] However, the military capability of Mittani cannot have lasted long after the death of Tushratta and the uncertain reign of his son, Kurtiwaza. By the end of the 14th century BCE, Mittani was all but a fading memory.

On point three, it is clear that Tushratta died shortly after the end of Akhenaten's reign, as a direct result of the military onslaught of Suppiluliuma against Mittani. Unless a case could be made that biblical Cushan = Tushratta (a Cush/Tush relationship could certainly be entertained), then the death of Tushratta provides a *terminus a quo* for the timeframe of Cushan's engagement against the Israelites. This makes even more sense when you realize that Tushratta, who had ruled since the days of Amenhotep III, had inherited the Egypto-Mittanian treaty initially negotiated during the reigns of Tuthmosis IV and Artatama. Although "Egyptian control of [Syria and Canaan] had ceased for all practical purposes" during the reigns of Amenhotep III and Akhenaten,[129] Tushratta had tried repeatedly to maintain his "brotherhood" with Akhenaten, especially in the face of continued Hittite expansion. However, as A. Goetze observes,

> Tushratta may have hoped for more active assistance, and, when none was forthcoming, his feelings toward the pharaoh became increasingly cool. His three extant letters to Ameno-phis IV [Akhenaten] show a growing animosity, and it may well be that after the third the correspondence was actually discontinued.[130]

We must remember that Tushratta's disgust with Egypt's inability to respond to the deteriorating situation in Syria during the reign of Akhenaten led to a breakdown of the Egyptian/Mittani "brotherhood." Late in Tushratta's reign, this would have given the Mittanis reason enough to pursue territories farther south in Canaan, since they had lost Syria to the Hittites and their eastern territories to the Assyrians, and their anger burned against Egypt for sleeping through it all. But it is doubtful that Tushratta himself could have launched such a campaign

---

128 Goetze, "Struggle" 1-20.
129 Ibid. 11.
130 Ibid. 7-8.

into Canaan, since during most of his reign, particularly the latter years up to the time of his death, he was either engaging the Hittites or hiding from them. Thus, it is entirely plausible that after the death of Tushratta, a subsequent Mittani king could have made forays into Canaan, thereby becoming the oppressor of Israel in Judges 3:7-11. After Tushratta, the record of activities in and around Mittani, including the number and names of subsequent rulers, is confused.[131] It is possible that during this uncertain period a Mittani king named Cushan (or something even roughly equivalent to it) could have launched a military action into Canaan against the Israelites.[132]

All of this leads to a precise historical synchronism between Judges 3:7-11 and the history of the Near East during the late Eighteenth Dynasty of Egypt if, and only if, Tuthmosis IV was the Pharaoh of the Exodus. If the biblical phrase "Cushan of [the caste of the] Rishathaim, king of Aram-Naharaim," refers to a Mittani king, and if Cushan is not Tushratta but a subsequent king, and if such a Mittani military campaign as described in Judges 3:7-11 could only have occurred before the end of the 14th fourteenth century BCE when the Kingdom of Mittani collapsed, then a very narrow slice of time is available for the judge Othniel to have defeated a Mittani king named Cushan. The chronology of events is computed in this manner:

(a)   Exodus Pharaoh Tuthmosis IV dies in the *yam suph.*

(b   Forty years later, in about the second year of Akhenaten's reign, Joshua leads the Israelites into Canaan for a series of military campaigns lasting seven years (ending about year nine of Akhenaten).

---

131 Ibid. 1-20.
132 It is also possible that the biblical reference to Cushan in Judges 3:7-11 is to a city-state king within the Mittani sphere, and not the king of the entire Mittani Kingdom (or what was left of it after the death of Tushratta). In this case a reasonable translation would be "Cushan of [the caste of] the Rishathaim, a king [from the region] of Aram-Naharaim." Such a city-state king living during the time of Tushratta would still have been prevented from attacking targets in Canaan because of the realities of Hittite expansion and the fact of the traditional Egyptian ownership of the southern Levant. However, in the ensuing years after Tushratta's death such a move would have been possible in the light of the stabilization of the Hittite annexation of Syria and the realization that Egypt had lost either its desire or ability to act in the region.

(c)   Shortly after the era of the Israelite Judges begins (say, ten
      years later = early in the reign of Tutankhamun and after
      the death of Tushratta), Cushan the Mittani oppresses the
      wayward Israelites, only to be defeated eight years later by
      Othniel (about the time of Tutankhamun's death).

The potential timeframe for Cushan's oppression of the Israelites in
Canaan is blocked on the early end by Tushratta's death and on the other
end by the demise of the Mittani Kingdom (see Figure 8). If the placement
of the Exodus is moved back just one pharaonic reign from Tuthmosis IV
to Amenhotep II, then the historical synchronism disappears because it
would place the Cushan oppression squarely in the reigns of Akhenaten
and Tushratta, at a time when the Mittanians still maintained hopeful
relations with their Egyptian "brothers," and/or Tushratta was "up to his
eyeballs" in Hittite aggression, making a Mittani military advance into
Canaan all but impossible. Placing the Exodus at the end of the reign of
Tuthmosis IV provides an adequate historical context for the placement
of Cushan's oppression of Israel. Also, the time window defined by the
terminus a quo and *terminus ad quem* for Mittanian military activity
in Canaanite territory is so slender as to reinforce the identification of
Tuthmosis IV as the only viable candidate for Pharaoh of the Exodus.

CONCLUSION AND RECOMMENDATIONS

If the biblical Exodus scenario took place during Egypt's Eighteenth
Dynasty, then the impact of those dramatic events upon Egypt should
make one particular chronological placement fit the history of Egypt
better than any other. The placement of the Exodus that creates the
greatest number of historical synchronisms between the Bible and
Egyptian history is in proximity with the death of Tuthmosis IV at
the height of the Eighteenth Dynasty. While other placements allow
potential synchronisms before the Exodus proper, only an Exodus
contemporaneous with the end of the reign of Tuthmosis IV provides
an adequate context for the predicted impacts of the Exodus core events
upon Egypt. While this placement would require slight adjustments to
accepted Egyptian and/or biblical chronologies in order to conform to
a strict mid-15th century BCE Exodus, the number of years needed to

accomplish such is very small. However, a biblical corrective to the Egyptian chronology would be, in my opinion, the recommended course (see Appendix Four).

The Reigns of the Egyptian Kings of the 18th Dynasty
in Regnal and Dynasty Years with Select Biblical Events
Using Tuthmosis IV as the Pharaoh of the Exodus
(Briggs Weighted-Average Chronology[1])

	LENGTH OF REIGN	DYNASTY YEARS	BIBLICAL CHRONOLOGY
2nd Intermediate Period (Hyksos)	(100 years)	(0-100)	Joseph in Egypt y_r43 Jacob in Egypt Israelites in Egypt
Amosis I	(24 years)	(0-24)	y_d13 anti-Asiatic Pharaoh and policies arise in Egypt
Amenhotep I	(21 years)	(24-45)	
Tuthmosis I	(12 years)	(45-57)	
Tuthmosis II	(10 years)	(57-67)	
Hatshepsut*	(21* years)	(67-88*)	y_d78 birth of Moses
Tuthmosis III	(54 years)	(67-121)	y_d118 Moses flees Egypt
Amenhotep II	(26 years)	(121-147)	
Tuthmosis IV	(11 years)	(147-158)	y_d158 Moses leads Exodus
Amenhotep III	(38 years)	(158-196)	
Amenhotep IV (Akhenaten)	(17 years)	(196-213)	y_d198 death of Moses Conquest begins
Smenkhkare**	(2** years)	(211-213**)	
Tutankhamun	(9 years)	(213-222)	
Ay	(4 years)	(222-226)	
Horemheb	(28 years)	(226-254)	
18th Dynasty TOTAL	(254 years)	(254 years)	

[1] P. Briggs, *Testing the Factuality of the Conquest of Ai Narrative in the Book of Joshua* (Doctoral Dissertation, Newburgh: Trinity Theological Seminary, 2001) 39.
*co-regency with Tuthmosis III
**co-regency with Akhenaten

Table 7.

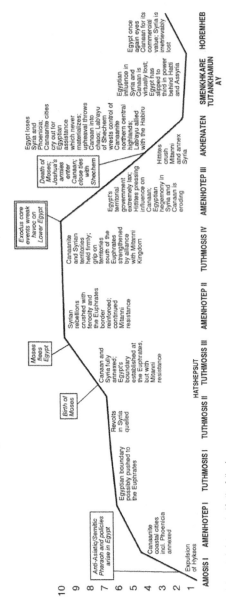

Figure 7. Several facts support the identification of Tuthmosis IV as the Exodus pharaoh, including: a) upon the death of Tuthmosis IV, Egypt begins to suffer hegemonic disintegration in Canaan and Syria, as predicted on the basis of the Exodus core events; b) forty years after the death of Tuthmosis IV, during Akhenaten's reign, Egyptian presence in Canaan was at a low ebb, making it doubtful that Joshua would have encountered any Egyptian interference during the Conquest, as implied by the book of Joshua; c) this is the only placement of the Exodus allowing an association between Joshua and Labayu of Shechem.

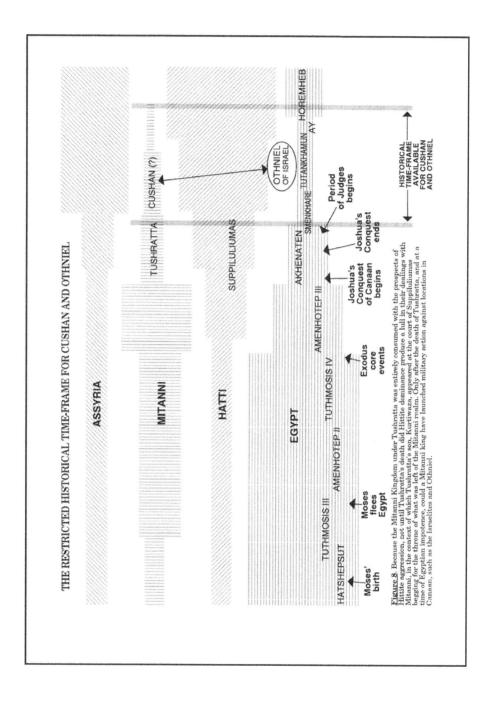

Figure 8. Because the Mitanni Kingdom under Tushratta was entirely consumed with the prospects of Hittite aggression, not until Tushratta's death did Hittite dominance produce a lull in their dealings with Mitanni. In the context of which Tushratta's son, Kurtiwaza, appeared at the court of Suppiluliumas begging for the throne of what was left of the Mitanni realm. Only after the death of Tushratta, and at a time of Egyptian impotence, could a Mitanni king have launched military action against locations in Canaan, such as the Israelites and Othniel.

Additional Tables and Figures

—ॐ—
The Reigns of the Egyptian Kings of the 18th and 19th Dynasties
in Regnal and Dynasty Years with Select Biblical Events
Using Rameses II as the Pharaoh of the Exodus
(with Exodus Dated Early in the Reign of Rameses II)
(Low Chronology[1])

	LENGTH OF REIGN	DYNASTY YEARS	BIBLICAL CHRONOLOGY
18th Dynasty:			Joseph in Egypt
			y.66 Jacob in Egypt
Hatshepsut*	(22* years)	(71-93*)	Israel in Egypt
Tuthmosis III	(54 years)	(71-125)	
Amenhotep II	(25 years)	(125-150)	
Tuthmosis IV	(10 years)	(150-160)	
Amenhotep III	(38 years)	(160-198)	
Amenhotep IV (Akhenaten)	(16 years)	(198-214)	y.201 birth of Moses
Smenkhkare**	(2** years)	(212-214**)	
Tutankhamun	(9 years)	(214-223)	
Ay	(4 years)	(223-227)	
Horemheb	(28 years)	(227-255)	y.241 Moses flees Egypt
19th Dynasty:			
Rameses I	(1 year)	(0-1)	
Seti I	(15 years)	(1-16)	y.26 Moses leads Exodus
Rameses II	(66 years)	(16-82)	y.66 death of Moses
Merneptah	(10 years)	(82-92)	Conquest begins
Rameses III	(31 years)	(2-33)	

[1] I. Shaw and P. Nicholson, Chronology, in *The Dictionary of Ancient Egypt* (1550, London), 811.
*co-regency with Tuthmosis III
**co-regency with Akhenaten

Table 8.

**The Reigns of the Egyptian Kings of the 18th Dynasty
in Regnal and Dynasty Years with Select Biblical Events
Using Rameses II as the Pharaoh of the Exodus
(with Exodus Dated to the Mid-Reign of Rameses II)
(Low Chronology[1])**

	LENGTH OF REIGN	DYNASTY YEARS	BIBLICAL CHRONOLOGY
18th Dynasty:			Joseph in Egypt
Hatshepsut*	(22* years)	(71-93*)	y$_d$89 Jacob in Egypt
			Israel in Egypt
Tuthmosis III	(54 years)	(71-125)	
Amenhotep II	(25 years)	(125-150)	
Tuthmosis IV	(10 years)	(150-160)	
Amenhotep III	(38 years)	(160-198)	
Amenhotep IV (Akhenaten)	(16 years)	(198-214)	
Smenkhkare**	(2** years)	(212-214**)	
Tutankhamun	(9 years)	(214-223)	
Ay	(4 years)	(223-227)	y$_d$224 birth of Moses
Horemheb	(28 years)	(227-255)	
19th Dynasty:			
Rameses I	(1 year)	(0-1)	
Seti I	(15 years)	(1-16)	y$_d$9 Moses flees Egypt
Rameses II	(66 years)	(16-82)	y$_d$49 Moses leads Exodus
Merneptah	(10 years)	(82-92)	y$_d$89 death of Moses
			Conquest begins
Amenmessu	(3 years)	(92-95)	

[1] I. Shaw and P. Nicholson, Chronology, in *The Dictionary of Ancient Egypt* (1995, London), 311.
*co-regency with Tuthmosis III
**co-regency with Akhenaten

Table 9.

**The Reigns of the Egyptian Kings of the 18th and 19th Dynasties
in Regnal and Dynasty Years with Select Biblical Events
Using Rameses II as the Pharaoh of the Exodus
(with Exodus Dated to the Death of Rameses II) (Low Chronology[1])**

	LENGTH OF REIGN	DYNASTY YEARS	BIBLICAL CHRONOLOGY
18th Dynasty:			
Hatshepsut*	(22* years)	(71-93*)	
Tuthmosis III	(54 years)	(71-125)	Joseph in Egypt y$_d$122 Jacob in Egypt Israel in Egypt
Amenhotep II	(25 years)	(125-150)	
Tuthmosis IV	(10 years)	(150-160)	
Amenhotep III	(38 years)	(160-198)	
Amenhotep IV (Akhenaten)	(16 years)	(198-214)	
Smenkhkare**	(2** years)	(212-214**)	
Tutankhamun	(9 years)	(214-223)	
Ay	(4 years)	(223-227)	
Horemheb	(28 years)	(227-255)	
19th Dynasty:			
Rameses I	(1 year)	(0-1)	
Seti I	(15 years)	(1-16)	y$_d$2 birth of Moses
Rameses II	(66 years)	(16-82)	y$_d$42 Moses flees Egypt y$_d$82 Moses leads Exodus
Merneptah	(10 years)	(82-92)	
Amenmessu	(3 years)	(92-95)	
Seti II	(6 years)	(95-101)	
Saptah	(6 years)	(101-107)	
Tausret	(2 years)	(107-109)	
19th Dynasty TOTAL	(109 years)	(109 years)	
20th Dynasty:			
Sethnakhte	(2 years)	(0-2)	
Rameses III	(31 years)	(2-33)	y$_d$13 death of Moses Conquest begins

[1] I. Shaw and P. Nicholson, Chronology, in *The Dictionary of Ancient Egypt* (1995, London), 311.
*co-regency with Tuthmosis III
**co-regency with Akhenaten

Table 10.

**The Reigns of the Egyptian Kings of the 18th Dynasty
in Regnal and Dynasty Years
(High Chronology[1])**

	LENGTH OF REIGN	DYNASTY YEARS
Amosis I	(24 years)	(0-24)
Amenhotep I	(20 years)	(24-44)
Tuthmosis I	(13 years)	(44-57)
Tuthmosis II	(8 years)	(57-65)
Hatshepsut*	(21* years)	(65-86*)
Tuthmosis III	(54 years)	(65-119)
Amenhotep II	(25 years)	(119-144)
Tuthmosis IV	(8 years)	(144-152)
Amenhotep III	(38 years)	(152-190)
Amenhotep IV (Akhenaten)	(17 years)	(190-207)
Smenkhkare	(3 years)	(207-210)
Tutankhamun	(9 years)	(210-219)
Ay	(4 years)	(219-223)
Horemheb	(28 years)	(223-251)
TOTAL	(251 years)	(251 years)

[1] W.C. Hayes: Chronological Tables (A) Egypt, in *Cambridge Ancient History*, Vol. II, Part 2 (1975), 1038.
*co-regency with Tuthmosis III

Table 11.

The Reigns of the Egyptian Kings of the 18th Dynasty in Regnal and Dynasty Years (Low Chronology[1])

	LENGTH OF REIGN	DYNASTY YEARS
Amosis I	(25 years)	(0-25)
Amenhotep I	(21 years)	(24-46)
Tuthmosis I	(12 years)	(46-58)
Tuthmosis II	(13 years)	(58-71)
Hatshepsut*	(22* years)	(71-93*)
Tuthmosis III	(54 years)	(71-125)
Amenhotep II	(25 years)	(125-150)
Tuthmosis IV	(10 years)	(150-160)
Amenhotep III	(38 years)	(160-198)
Amenhotep IV (Akhenaten)	(16 years)	(198-214)
Smenkhkare**	(2** years)	(212-214**)
Tutankhamun	(9 years)	(214-223)
Ay	(4 years)	(223-227)
Horemheb	(28 years)	(227-255)
TOTAL	(255 years)	(255 years)

[1] K.A. Kitchen: Egypt, History of (Chronology), in *The Anchor Bible Dictionary*, Vol 2, ed by D.N. Freedman (New York: Doubleday, 1992), 322-31.
*co-regency with Tuthmosis III
**co-regency with Akhenaten

Table 12.

**The Reigns of the Egyptian Kings of the 18th Dynasty
in Regnal and Dynasty Years
(Wente & Van Siclen Chronology[1])**

	LENGTH OF REIGN	DYNASTY YEARS
Amosis I	(24 years)	(0-24)
Amenhotep I	(22 years)	(24-46)
Tuthmosis I	(6 years)	(46-52)
Tuthmosis II	(14 years)	(52-66)
Hatshepsut*	(20* years)	(66-86*)
Tuthmosis III	(54 years)	(66-120)
Amenhotep II	(31 years)	(120-151)
Tuthmosis IV	(33 years)	(151-184)
Amenhotep III	(37 years)	(184-221)
Amenhotep IV (Akhenaten)	(15 years)	(221-236)
Smenkhkare**	(2** years)	(234-236**)
Tutankhamun	(9 years)	(236-245)
Ay	(4 years)	(245-249)
Horemheb	(28 years)	(249-277)
TOTAL	(277 years)	(277 years)

[1] E. Wente and C. Van Siclen III: A Chronology of the New Kingdom, in *Studies in Honor of George R. Hughes* January 12, 1977, *Studies in Ancient Oriental Civilization* No. 39 (Chicago: The Oriental Institute, 1977), 217-261.
*co-regency with Tuthmosis III
**co-regency with Akhenaten

Table 13.

The Reigns of the Egyptian Kings of the 18th Dynasty in Regnal and Dynasty Years with Select Biblical Events Using Tuthmosis IV as the Pharaoh of the Exodus (High Chronology[1])

	LENGTH OF REIGN	DYNASTY YEARS	BIBLICAL CHRONOLOGY
2nd Intermediate Period (Hyksos)	(100 years)	(0-100)	Joseph in Egypt y_a37 Jacob in Egypt Israelites in Egypt
Amosis I	(24 years)	(0-24)	y_a7 anti-Asiatic Pharaoh and policies arise
Amenhotep I	(20 years)	(24-44)	in Egypt
Tuthmosis I	(13 years)	(44-57)	
Tuthmosis II	(8 years)	(57-65)	
Hatshepsut*	(21* years)	(65-86*)	y_a72 birth of Moses
Tuthmosis III	(54 years)	(65-119)	y_a112 Moses flees Egypt
Amenhotep II	(25 years)	(119-144)	
Tuthmosis IV	(8 years)	(144-152)	y_a152 Moses leads Exodus
Amenhotep III	(38 years)	(152-190)	
Amenhotep IV (Akhenaten)	(17 years)	(190-207)	y_a192 death of Moses Conquest begins
Smenkhkare	(3 years)	(207-210)	
Tutankhamun	(9 years)	(210-219)	
Ay	(4 years)	(219-223)	
Horemheb	(28 years)	(223-251)	
18th Dynasty TOTAL	(251 years)	(251 years)	

[1] W.C. Hayes: Chronological Tables (A) Egypt, in *Cambridge Ancient History*, Vol. II, Part 2 (1975), 1038.
*co-regency with Tuthmosis III

Table 14.

**The Reigns of the Egyptian Kings of the 18th Dynasty
in Regnal and Dynasty Years with Select Biblical Events
Using Tuthmosis IV as the Pharaoh of the Exodus
(Low Chronology[1])**

	LENGTH OF REIGN	DYNASTY YEARS	BIBLICAL CHRONOLOGY
2nd Intermediate Period (Hyksos)	(100 years)	(0-100)	Joseph in Egypt y_d45 Jacob in Egypt Israel in Egypt
Amosis I	(25 years)	(0-25)	y_d15 anti-Asiatic Pharaoh and policies arise
Amenhotep I	(21 years)	(24-46)	in Egypt
Tuthmosis I	(12 years)	(46-58)	
Tuthmosis II	(13 years)	(58-71)	
Hatshepsut*	(22* years)	(71-93*)	y_e80 birth of Moses
Tuthmosis III	(54 years)	(71-125)	y_d120 Moses flees Egypt
Amenhotep II	(25 years)	(125-150)	
Tuthmosis IV	(10 years)	(150-160)	y_d160 Moses leads Exodus
Amenhotep III	(38 years)	(160-198)	
Amenhotep IV (Akhenaten)	(16 years)	(198-214)	y_d200 death of Moses Conquest begins
Smenkhkare**	(2** years)	(212-214**)	
Tutankhamun	(9 years)	(214-223)	
Ay	(4 years)	(223-227)	
Horemheb	(28 years)	(227-255)	
18th Dynasty TOTAL	(255 years)	(255 years)	

[1] K.A. Kitchen: Egypt, History of (Chronology), in *The Anchor Bible Dictionary*, Vol 2, ed by D.N. Freedman (New York: Doubleday, 1992), 322-31.
*co-regency with Tuthmosis III
**co-regency with Akhenaten

Table 15.

**The Reigns of the Egyptian Kings of the 18th Dynasty
in Regnal and Dynasty Years with Select Biblical Events
Using Tuthmosis IV as the Pharaoh of the Exodus
(Wente & Van Siclen Chronology[1])**

	LENGTH OF REIGN	DYNASTY YEARS	BIBLICAL CHRONOLOGY
2nd Intermediate Period (Hyksos)	(100 years)	(0-100)	Joseph in Egypt y_d69 Jacob in Egypt Israelites in Egypt
Amosis I	(24 years)	(0-24)	
Amenhotep I	(22 years)	(24-46)	y_d39 anti-Asiatic Pharaoh and policies arise
Tuthmosis I	(6 years)	(46-52)	in Egypt
Tuthmosis II	(14 years)	(52-66)	
Hatshepsut*	(20* years)	(66-86*)	
Tuthmosis III	(54 years)	(66-120)	y_d104 birth of Moses
Amenhotep II	(31 years)	(120-151)	y_d144 Moses flees Egypt
Tuthmosis IV	(33 years)	(151-184)	y_d184 Moses leads Exod.
Amenhotep III	(37 years)	(184-221)	
Amenhotep IV (Akhenaten)	(15 years)	(221-236)	y_d224 death of Moses Conquest begins
Smenkhkare**	(2** years)	(234-236**)	
Tutankhamun	(9 years)	(236-245)	
Ay	(4 years)	(245-249)	
Horemheb	(28 years)	(249-277)	
18th Dynasty TOTAL	(277 years)	(277 years)	

[1] E. Wente and C. Van Siclen III: A Chronology of the New Kingdom, in *Studies in Honor of George R. Hughes* January 12, 1977, *Studies in Ancient Oriental Civilization* No. 39 (Chicago: The Oriental Institute, 1977), 217-261.
*co-regency with Tuthmosis III
**co-regency with Akhenaten

Table 16.

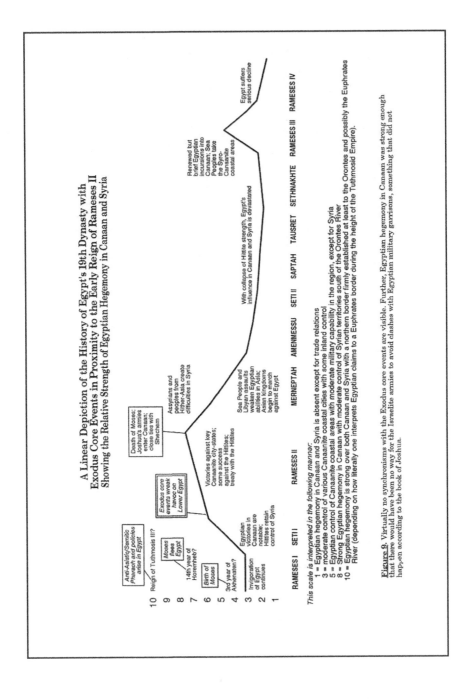

A Linear Depiction of the History of Egypt's 19th Dynasty with Exodus Core Events in Proximity to the Early Reign of Rameses II Showing the Relative Strength of Egyptian Hegemony in Canaan and Syria

This scale is interpreted in the following manner:

1 = Egyptian hegemony in Canaan and Syria is absent except for trade relations
3 = moderate control of various Canaanite coastal cities with some inland control
5 = Egyptian control of Canaanite coastal areas with moderate military capability in the region, except for Syria
8 = Strong Egyptian hegemony in Canaan with moderate control of Syrian territories south of the Orontes River
10 = Egyptian hegemony is strong over both Canaan and Syria with a northern border firmly established at least to the Orontes and possibly the Euphrates River (depending on how literally one interprets Egyptian claims to a Euphrates border during the height of the Tuthmosid Empire).

Figure 9. Virtually no synchronisms with the Exodus core events are visible. Further, Egyptian hegemony in Canaan was strong enough that there would have been no way for the Israelite armies to avoid clashes with Egyptian military garrisons, something that did not happen according to the book of Joshua.

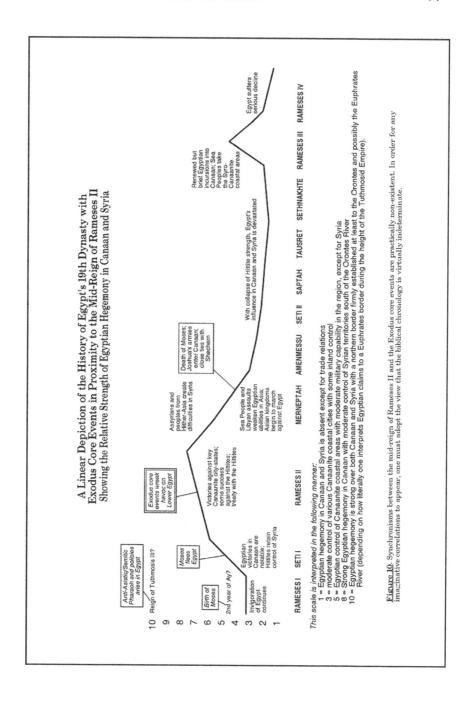

Figure 10. Synchronisms between the mid-reign of Rameses II and the Exodus core events are practically non-existent. In order for any imaginative correlations to appear, one must adopt the view that the biblical chronology is virtually indeterminate.

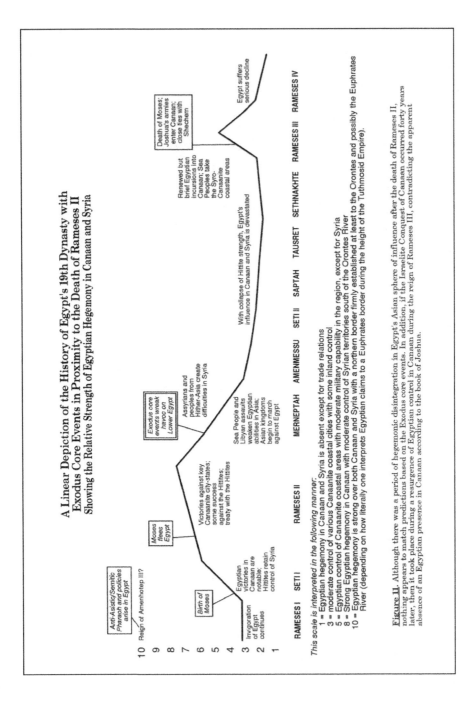

Figure 11. Although there was a period of hegemonic disintegration in Egypt's Asian sphere of influence after the death of Rameses II, nothing appears to match predictions based on the Exodus core events. In addition, if the Israelite Conquest of Canaan occurred forty years later, then it took place during a resurgence of Egyptian control in Canaan during the reign of Rameses III, contradicting the apparent absence of an Egyptian presence in Canaan according to the book of Joshua.

APPENDIX TWO

The Length of the Israelite
Sojourn in Egypt

—ₘ—

The length of the Israelite sojourn in Egypt significantly impacts a
number of key chronological issues. Among these issues are: (a)
the timeframe and cultural context for the life of the Hebrew patriarch,
Abraham; (b) the proposed identification of the Early Bronze Age cities
of Bab edh-Dhra and Numeira with biblical Sodom and Gomorrah; (c)
the identification of the Egyptian Dynasty during which Joseph served
as vizier; (d) the placement of the Exodus events in either the Eighteenth
or Nineteenth Dynasty of Egypt.

As much argumentation as I have examined relative to the length of
the Israelite sojourn in Egypt,[133] I am convinced that there is only one

---

133 It is worth noting that scholars seem to use either a short or long Israelite sojourn in Egypt
depending upon the needs of their particular theories, with but little critical analysis as to
which length of sojourn is best supported by the evidence. For example, while K.A. Kitchen
postulates a much-abbreviated timespan (on the order of 280 years or so) for the (literal) 480
years of Exodus 12:40 in order to accommodate his preference for a mid-13th century BCE
date for the Exodus, he readily adopts a long, 400-plus-year Egyptian sojourn to avoid placing Joseph in the middle of the Eighteenth Dynasty where he obviously does not belong. See
K.A. Kitchen, *The Bible in Its World* (Downers Grove: InterVarsity, 1978) 74-76.

B.G. Wood, who holds to an early, mid-15th century BCE Exodus date, assumes a long
sojourn in Egypt because he needs to push the date of Abraham's entrance into Canaan as far
back as possible to preserve some hope of identifying Bab edh-Dhra and Numeira as Sodom
and Gomorrah. See B.G. Wood, "The Discovery of the Sin Cities of Sodom and Gomorrah,"
BS 12.3 (1999) 66-80. It is interesting to observe that this article includes a photograph of Dr.
Wood standing next to an information sign placed at Bab edh-Dhra by the Jordanian Ministry
of Tourism and Antiquities stating that the main (fortified) occupation of the town was
destroyed about 2400 BCE toward the end of EB III, more than 300 years before the earliest
possible date that Abraham and Lot could have entered Canaan.

In my opinion, the best treatment of the subject in support of the long Egyptian sojourn scenario is P.J. Ray, Jr., "The Duration of the Israelite Sojourn in Egypt," *BS* 17.2 (2004) 33-44.
This is the revised version of an article that originally appeared in *AUSS* 24 (1986) 231-248.

fragment of evidence—and that highly questionable—in support of a long (430-year) sojourn in Egypt, i.e., Exodus 12:40 in the Masoretic Text: "Now the length of time the Israelite people lived in Egypt was 430 years." Yet many conservative scholars, particularly evangelicals, cling to the 430 years of Exodus 12:40(MT) as if the evidence overwhelmingly favored it. But in fact, practically all other conceivable lines of evidence point to a short (215-year) sojourn in Egypt, clearly revealing that the reading of the Masoretic Text in Exodus 12:40 is the result of a scribal omission made sometime before or during the Middle Ages (ca. 1000 CE).

Other witnesses to the text of Exodus 12:40—namely, the Samaritan Pentateuch and the Septuagint (LXX)—attest to the following reading: "Now the length of time the Israelite people lived in Egypt and in Canaan was 430 years." Both the Alexandrian-Jewish chronographer, Demetrius (before 200 BCE) and the Jewish-Roman historian, Josephus (1st century CE) clearly support this reading of Exodus 12:40.[134] Josephus writes that "[the Israelites] left Egypt....four hundred and thirty years after our forefather Abraham came into Canaan, but two hundred and fifteen years only after Jacob removed into Egypt."[135] Translator Whiston's footnote on this passage from Josephus is instructive:

> Why our Masorete copy so groundlessly abridges this account in Exod. 12:40, as to ascribe 430 years to the sole peregrination of the Israelites in Egypt when it is clear even by that Masorete chronology elsewhere, as well as from the express text itself, in the Samaritan [Pentateuch], Septuagint and Josephus, that they sojourned in Egypt but half that time—and that by consequence, the other half of their peregrination was in the land of Canaan, before they came into Egypt—is hard to say.[136]

Even the apostle Paul in Galatians 3:17 supports a short Egyptian sojourn by affirming that from "the promises....spoken to Abraham" to the giving of the Mosaic Law, the total elapsed time was 430 years—again, 215 years in Canaan (Abraham to Jacob) and 215 years in Egypt (Jacob

---

134 Finegan, *Chronology* 204-205.
135 Flavius Josephus, *The Antiquities of the Jews* (2.15.2) in *The Works of Josephus: New Updated Edition*, tr. by W. Whiston (Peabody: Hendrickson, 1987) 74-75.
136 See translator Whiston's footnote on Josephus, *Antiquities* (2.15.2) 75.

to Moses). From an historical point of view, Paul's commentary provides evidence for the state of the text of Exodus 12:40 in the mid-1st century CE, which included both locatives, Egypt and Canaan, as components of the Israelite sojourn. Further, to imply that Paul was only familiar with the LXX reading as a backdrop for Galatians 3:17 is ludicrous; Paul's extensive training as a "Hebrew of the Hebrews" (Philippians 3:4-6) would have certainly given him an intimate knowledge of the then-extant Hebrew text of Exodus.

Thus, from an evangelical point of view, only two distinct possibilities exist to account for Paul's clear support of a 430-year period from Abraham to Moses (= short sojourn in Egypt):

(a)   At the time Paul wrote Galatians, both the Hebrew and LXX texts of Exodus 12:40 read "in Egypt and Canaan....430 years," suggesting that the Hebrew textual tradition leading to the much later Masoretic Text suffered the omission of "Canaan" after the time of Paul (and probably much later).

(b)   If the variant readings of Exodus 12:40 existed in the 1st century CE, then the Holy Spirit obviously inspired Paul to select the correct one, i.e., "in Egypt and Canaan....430 years."

When you add to these points the fact that the Masoretic genealogies from Abraham to Jacob and from Jacob to Moses fit best into two 215-year periods,[137] the best conclusion appears to discredit a long sojourn in Egypt. J. Finegan's gentle rejection of a long sojourn in Egypt is more than kind,[138] for an application of even the most basic logic to the available data explodes the notion that the Israelites were in Egypt for 430 years.

OBJECTIONS TO A SHORT SOJOURN

Just to be fair, though, I want to deal with a handful of issues brought up by J.P. Ray in his defense of the longer sojourn scenario (see the

---

137   Finegan, *Chronology* 203-206.
138   Ibid.

publication information in footnote 133). He certainly understands the points in favor of a short sojourn, but dismisses it in favor of the 430-year sojourn for several reasons. I will answer each in turn.

First, he suggests that possibly since the time of the LXX (3rd century BCE) "there has been a tradition that the 430 years in Exodus 12:40… represent only 215 years of actual years of Israelite sojourn in Egypt, with the other 215 years representing the sojourn in Canaan." But such a take is slanted toward his view, as if the short sojourn idea were simply an "alternate" tradition to the longer one. Realistically, the long sojourn tradition seems to be purely a late idea spawned by a scribal error leading to the reading of Exodus 12:40 in the MT. Who held to a long sojourn before that? Not many, as far as I can tell.

Second, Ray suggests that Josephus "provides a divided testimony." In spite of the fact that Josephus is so adamant about the short sojourn in his *Antiquities* (2.15.2), with his *Contra Apion* (1.14) giving full support to this, Ray cites another passage in *Antiquities* (2.9.1) that, in his opinion, seems to support the MT: "And four hundred years did they spend under these afflictions…" Clearly this reflects the 400 years of Genesis 15:13 and might seem to suggest a 400-year sojourn, but not necessarily; Josephus may merely be skimming over the issue with the precision of the Genesis passage oversimplified or ignored (see the next paragraph). But just as Genesis 15:13 must be understood in the light of other biblical texts, such as Exodus 12:40 (LXX) and Galatians 3:17, so the *Antiquities* 2.9.1 passage should be understood in the light of the *Antiquities* 2.15.2 passage which, for Josephus, is definitive on the issue. In the same paragraph, Ray points out that even Rabbinic tradition supports a short Egyptian sojourn, citing *Seder* 'Ôlām (2nd century) and Rashi (11th century), suggesting also that the Midrash is vague on the issue. So, nothing here really favors the long sojourn.

Third, Ray attempts to sell the idea that the "NT also appears to be divided on the subject." But I would respond, Appears divided to whom? He cites Acts 7:6-7 and 13:17-20. But the Acts 7 passage deals with Genesis 15:13, not Exodus 12:40. Genesis 15:13 says, "Then Yahweh said to him, 'Know for certain that your descendants will be strangers in a country not their own, and they will be enslaved and mistreated four hundred years.'" The meaning is not vague here. The descendants of Abraham would have two things happen during a period of 400 years: (a) they would be strangers in a country not their own (Canaan!), and (b) they would be enslaved and mistreated (in Egypt!). Where is the long Egyptian sojourn? The Acts 13 passage says, "The God of the people of Israel chose our fathers; he made the people prosper during their stay in Egypt, with mighty power he led them out of that country, he endured their conduct for about forty years in the desert, he overthrew seven nations in Canaan and gave their land to his people as their inheritance. All this took about 450 years. After this, God gave them judges until the time of Samuel the prophet."

Let's analyze this…over a period of 450 years God did several things: (a) he chose our fathers (the Hebrew Patriarchs), (b) he made them prosper in Egypt, (c) he led them out of Egypt, (d) he put up with them in the wilderness, and (e) he overthrew the nations in Canaan and gave that land to the Israelites. There is absolutely nothing here demanding a long sojourn in Egypt, especially if the "fathers" included Abraham. The Apostle Paul's statement in Galatians 3:17 is *the* definitive New Testament passage on the issue. And Ray agrees that Paul follows the LXX rendering of Exodus 12:40! The New Testament is not divided on the issue at all—it is a short (215-year) Israelite sojourn in Egypt all the way.

Fourth, he attempts to show a division on the issue among the Ante-Nicene Fathers, namely Tertullian (short sojourn) and Hippolytus (long sojourn). But the argument for a long sojourn here is not compelling and derives no final conclusion.

Fifth, Ray states that "the majority of ancient texts lend support to the long chronology (for the sojourn in Egypt alone). While this fact does not, of course, provide conclusive support for that chronology, it does indicate a direction of probability as to the original." However, Ray's use of the term "conclusive support" is terribly misleading. There is no line of reasoning that justifies the use of the term "conclusive" as a description of the evidence for a long sojourn chronology, even if tempered by a carefully placed negative disclaimer. To jump from that to the conclusion "it does indicate a direction of probability as to the original" is simply unwarranted.

The balance of Ray's argumentation is, frankly, insignificant. He simply attempts to rationalize what more clearly fits a short sojourn scenario. To be willing to argue in favor of this position, long sojourn supporters like Ray must have something else at stake that they desire to preserve at the expense of better logic and evidence. Indeed the following four ideas are what they generally want to hang onto, but these four ideas must be dismissed if one adopts a short Egyptian sojourn.

FOUR IDEAS THAT EVAPORATE
WITH A SHORT EGYPTIAN SOJOURN

If one adopts the short sojourn scenario (Jacob to Moses is approximately 215 years), then numerous conclusions about biblical chronology and its correspondence with ancient Near Eastern history and archaeology, which are based on a 430-year Israelite sojourn in Egypt, must be abandoned. Four significant ones are as follows:

1. *The placement of Abraham in the Intermediate Bronze Age (2350-1950 BCE; formerly Early Bronze IV and Middle Bronze I).*[139]
    If the Exodus occurred about 1446 BCE (based on the Masoretic Text of 1 Kings 6:1) or 1406 BCE (based on the LXX rendering of 1 Kings 6:1), then the earliest possible date for the entrance of Abraham into Canaan 430 years earlier would be the first half of the 19th nineteenth century BCE, which, by any stretch of the imagination, was well into Middle Bronze Age IIA. Thus, the idea so popular with evangelical scholars—that Abraham lived in the Intermediate Bronze Age—should be abandoned. Abraham was a resident of Canaan during the prosperous Middle Bronze Age IIA (now Middle Bronze I in many chronologies; 1950-1750 BCE).

---

139 The problem is not that most scholars try to place Abraham earlier than the Middle Bronze Age; they generally do not. It is simply that the long Israelite sojourn in Egypt assumed by some scholars forces the patriarch into the latter half of the Intermediate Bronze Age which is a considerably different cultural picture than the more stable and prosperous MB IIA (now MB I in many chronologies). Projecting an accurate historical/cultural context for Abraham depends on a more precise chronological placement. If the Egyptian sojourn of the Israelites is actually on the order of 215 years as the bulk of the evidence suggests, then there is no point in discussing Abraham in the light of Mesopotamian, Syrian, and Canaanite socio-cultural contexts earlier than MB IIA.

2. _The identification of Bab edh-Dhra and Numeira as Sodom and Gomorrah._[140] There have been numerous recent attempts to equate the Jordanian sites of Bab edh-Dhra and Numeira with the Sodom and Gomorrah of Genesis 13ff.

The biblical stories involving the "cities of the plain," including these two infamous locations, occurred in the days of Abraham and Lot. Since Sodom and Gomorrah were contemporaneous with these two patriarchs, then those sites must have been occupied and thriving during Middle Bronze Age IIA, the correct chronological placement of Abraham in Canaan. But since both Bab edh-Dhra and Numeira were destroyed toward the end of Early Bronze Age IV, no later than 2200 BCE,[141] they cannot remotely be associated with the careers of Abraham and Lot.[142] Furthermore, the biblical text tells us that Sodom was a walled town, for "Lot was sitting in the gateway of the city [Sodom]" (Genesis 19:1). Excavations at Bab edh-Dhra—the site most often identified as Sodom—reveal that its final walled phase was destroyed about 2400 BCE, toward the end of Early Bronze III.[143] The subsequent phase was an open settlement destroyed about 2200 BCE. After that, the site was abandoned. Thus, because both Bab edh-Dhra and Numeira were destroyed from three to five hundred years before Abraham entered Canaan, there is no hope of associating him with those Early Bronze Age towns. (Even if you assign to Abraham the earliest possible date for entering Canaan, say, about 2100 BCE, he would still arrive in the land three hundred years after the walled town of Bab edh-Dhra was destroyed.) Obviously, Sodom and Gomorrah remain unidentified.

---

140 Attempts to identify Bab edh-Dhra and Numeira as Sodom and Gomorrah abound in the recent literature. See B.G. Wood's recent _BS_ article titled "The Discovery of the Sin Cities of Sodom and Gomorrah" (cited above in note 133) for a good range of bibliographical references.

141 R.T. Schaub, "Bab edh-Dhra'," _NEAEHL_, vol. 1, E. Stern, ed. (Jerusalem and New York: Israel Exploration Society and Carta; Simon and Schuster, 1993) 130-136. See also M.D. Coogan, "Numeira 1981," _BASOR_ 255 (1984) 75-81.

142 Using a long, 430-year Israelite sojourn in Egypt, the earliest possible date for the birth of Abraham is about 2166 BCE, placing him in Canaan about a century later. See Finegan, _Chronology_ 202.

143 Schaub, "Bab edh-Dhra'" 130-136.

3. ***Joseph served as vizier of Egypt during the latter part of the Middle Kingdom (2000-1786 BCE).***[144] If Jacob's entrance into Egypt occurred approximately 215 years before the Exodus—as the bulk of the evidence suggests—then, given a mid-15th century BCE date for the Exodus events, Joseph served as Egyptian vizier no earlier than the early- to mid-17[th]century BCE, squarely in the middle of Egypt's Second Intermediate Period (ca. 1786-1570 BCE). Thus, Joseph's Egyptian career did not take place during the Middle Kingdom, as some scholars insist, but during the Hyksos Period when Semitic Asiatics from Canaan ruled Lower Egypt. While many scholars are convinced that the Hyksos Period is indeed the best context for Joseph based on socio-cultural data,[145] the fact of a short Egyptian sojourn for the Israelites rules out, on very solid chronological grounds, any earlier placement.

4. ***The Exodus occurred during the reign of Rameses II around 1270-1250 BCE***.[146] Advocates of a late (13th century BCE) date for the Exodus traditionally opt for a long (430-year) Israelite sojourn in Egypt. But they do so in violation of their own "logic," which treats the 480 (MT)/440 (LXX) years of 1 Kings 6:1 as a hyperbolic figure signifying twelve generations,[147] allowing them to shorten that time period enough to place the Exodus in the 13th century BCE. If, as they say, the 480-year figure of 1 Kings 6:1 must be reduced to only 300 years or fewer, then why do they insist that the 430 (MT) years of Exodus 12:40 is generally accurate? They must adopt the Masoretic figure of 430 years in Egypt because that is the only way they can keep Joseph out of the (very anti-Asiatic/Semitic) Eighteenth Dynasty, where he absolutely does not belong. Adding 430 years to 1270/1250 BCE puts Joseph in Egypt during the Second Intermediate Period under the reign of the Hyksos, where he fits perfectly

---

144 Since most advocates of an early, 15th-century BCE date for the Exodus seem uncritically to assume a long, 430-year sojourn in Egypt, Joseph invariably winds up in the latter part of Egypt's Middle Kingdom, usually in the Twelfth Dynasty. See C.F. Aling, *Egypt and Bible History* (Grand Rapids: Baker, 1981).

145 See discussions in Kitchen, *Bible in Its World* 74; Hoffmeier, *Israel in Egypt* 77-106; and Finegan, *Chronology* 213-224.

146 See discussions in Kitchen, *Bible in Its World* 75-91; Kitchen, *Pharaoh Triumphant* 70-71; and Hoffmeier, *Israel in Egypt* 107-163.

147 See the discussions in Hoffmeier, *Israel in Egypt* 122-126, and Finegan, *Chronology* 224-245.

However, since the evidence does not at all support a long sojourn in Egypt, but one of only 215 years, the placement of Joseph based on a 13th century BCE Exodus would be in the Eighteenth Dynasty during the reign of the great warrior-king, Tuthmosis III—an historical context entirely foreign to the Joseph story. Thus, the fact of a 215-year Israelite sojourn in Egypt militates against an Exodus during the reign of Rameses II and argues strongly in favor of a mid-15th century Exodus.

In summary, computing a biblical chronology based on a 430-year Israelite sojourn in Egypt is erroneous. Virtually every line of reasoning and evidence points to the factuality of a short, 215-year sojourn. The reality of the 215-year sojourn, in turn, categorically eliminates at least four widely held theories: (a) Abraham in the Intermediate Bronze Age, (b) Bab edh-Dhra and Numeira as Sodom and Gomorrah, (c) Joseph as vizier during the Egypt's Middle Kingdom, and (d) Rameses II as Pharaoh of the Exodus. Contrariwise, a 215-year Israelite sojourn in Egypt lends substantial support to the following: (a) Middle Bronze Age IIA as the correct socio-cultural context for the life of Abraham, (b) Sodom and Gomorrah as yet unidentified, (c) Joseph as vizier of Egypt during the Hyksos Period, and (d) the Exodus in the 15th century BCE during the Eighteenth Dynasty.

The Bible, History, and Objectivity

—〰—

Reality is seamless; history is not. History is sewn together in our minds by connecting fragments of the reality that we experience via our senses. And there is no possible way that human beings, individually or collectively, can even begin to observe all the nuances of reality; indeed much or most of reality escapes our notice. While the historian may attribute the winning of a great battle to the military genius of the victorious general, a peek at the undetected reality of it all might very well reveal that the losing army suffered defeat due to a plague of acute diarrhea (recall the plague of hemorrhoids that Yahweh brought upon the Philistines when they captured the Ark of the Covenant! [1 Samuel 5]). Indeed, the loss of a battle may be accounted by the historian as the result of any number of physical factors, while in reality it may have been the hand of God.

For some odd reason, historians and archaeologists alike (not to mention the majority of philosophers and scientists) meticulously avoid integrating the divine into their perceptions of the universe. Even when people of faith write history, they often seek to stroke the skepticism of their readers by sewing in patches of "rationalism," which suggest that "miracles," like the children of Israel crossing the Re(e)d Sea, could very well have been accomplished by a concert of converging natural phenomena. Just to mention the idea that God may have taken advantage of some localized climatological or geological occurrence to accomplish his purposes seems to make us feel better about the possibility that such stories may have some truth to them after all. Yet if God does exist, would he not be the most fundamental element of reality itself? Then why are some so eager to dismiss the clear work of his hand in the mortal dimension? And why should we suppose that our pathetically limited perceptions accurately represent the reality we so feebly observe?

I understand perfectly well the penchant of some historians to dismiss as much of the "supernatural" as possible. After all, logic and reason should prevail in our attempts to write about the past. But we must be careful about what we allow to pass for logic and reason. If God exists and he is the Creator of all and is actively involved in his universe, then it makes absolutely no sense to write him out of his own story. I find that in writing history, many historians are terribly illogical and unreasonable in their treatment of the biblical stories not only in disparaging the divine element, but also in dismissing the historicity of the people and events associated with divine activity. For example, not only is Abraham's interaction with his God, Yahweh, disbelieved, but also the historical existence of Abraham himself is denied.[148]

This kind of categorical dismissal of the historical character of the biblical narratives is, from a historiographical perspective, sheer nonsense. Such anti-biblical bias is clearly exposed when we examine how our understanding of history is pieced together from the extant records of the ancient Near East. The documents and inscriptions from which we derive our ancient Near Eastern "histories" are all, without exception, set within a mythological context amidst gods, goddesses, and demons, yet historians are accustomed to accept these ancient accounts as generally factual and their human characters as actual. If this were not the case, we would have no histories of ancient Egypt, Anatolia, or Mesopotamia. The stories of great Egyptian pharaohs like Tuthmosis III and Rameses II are inextricably bound to divine dimensions, yet no one denies the historical reality behind these characters, who, by their own proclamations, wore the mantle of divinity.

But often when historians and archaeologists approach the biblical stories, key characters—Abraham, Joseph, Moses, Joshua—and the

---

148   I cannot over-emphasize this point. Dismissing the historical factuality of biblical characters is not, nor has it ever been, a logical scholarly exercise. The fact that so many scholars are allowed to get away with such subjective nonsense casts a rather dismal light on the entire historical-critical community.

accomplishments attributed to them because of their relationship to Yahweh are called fictional, non-historical, or mythical. The reality of the human characters in Egyptian records is uncritically accepted, while the existence of the Israelite heroes is readily dismissed. Treating the biblical characters in this manner is historiographically unjustified, illogical, and unreasonable. And we must not be so irresponsible as to reject categorically the interaction of Yahweh, the biblical God of history, with these men and women of old. Indeed, the whirlwind may be the result of God's hand sweeping through reality, creating a vortex of observed phenomena which defies all human powers of observation and explanation. To the human witness, reality may evidence all manner of chaos, whereas the Bible allows us to see that the whirlwind is often shaped like the hand of God—but only for those who through Scripture have enough "distance" to observe from the divine perspective.

In dismissing the historical integrity of the Bible, some scholars are forced by their anti-biblical bias to postulate extremely late dates for the origin of biblical stories. But in doing so, they multiply their error and reveal their inability to exercise reasonable objectivity. One good example of this—and I could give dozens of others[149]—is the use of selective comparisons between segments of biblical narrative with cultural contexts that are much later in date than the face-value biblical chronology would suggest. J.K. Hoffmeier, in his excellent work *Israel in Egypt*, notes the glaring weakness of J. Van Seters' comparison of the Israelite crossing of the Jordan River during flood stage with Neo-Assyrian (ca. 8th century BCE) accounts of Sargon II and Ashurbanipal's crossing of the Tigris and Euphrates during the spring high-water season. Hoffmeier counters:

> Van Seters's treatment of this matter fails on two points. First, the spring of the year was the traditional time for kings to go to war in Israel (cf. 2 Sam. 11:2) as well as in Mesopotamia....Spring is also when the rivers, the Jordan as well as the Tigris and Euphrates, are at their highest levels because

---

149 See works such as Finkelstein and Na'aman, *Nomadism*; Lemche, *Prelude*; Finkelstein and Silberman, *Unearthed*; and Ahlstrom, *Ancient Palestine*. For potent refutations of this kind of hypercritical thinking, see W.G. Dever, *What Did the Biblical Writers Know and When Did They Know It?* (Grand Rapids/Cambridge, UK: Eerdmans, 2001); and K.A. Kitchen, *On the Reliability of the Old Testament* (Grand Rapids/Cambridge, UK: Eerdmans, 2003).

of melting snow from the mountains to the north. Secondly, the seemingly miraculous crossing of raging rivers by a king is well attested in earlier Near Eastern sources [such as] Hattusili I (ca. 1650 B.C.) [and] Sargon the Great (ca. 2371-2316 B.C.). Consequently, there is no basis for Van Seters's assertion. The river crossing in Joshua 3 by Israel's forces accurately reflects the seasonal realities of military life in the Near East throughout the three millennia B.C.[150]

Scholars like Van Seters are fond of comparing biblical materials with later (usually late Iron Age) Near Eastern texts and cultural settings for the purpose of supporting their thesis that the stories of the biblical patriarchs and origins of Israel were myths or fictions concocted by Jewish priests as late as the Persian, even Hellenistic, periods. Their disregard for objectivity is evidenced by the fact that they fail to make comparative analyses based on Near Eastern texts and cultural contexts of the third and second millennia BCE where, according to the biblical chronology, the events actually took place.

We must be careful to admit that human sensory observation, memory, and recall are, at best, only frayed pieces of the seamless fabric of reality. Thus, God is the sole objective observer of reality, because only his perspective allows a viewing of the seamless whole. When God represents reality, or a segment of it, that representation is perfectly true. And even if the divine representations provide only minute glimpses of past events, those glimpses are perfectly factual on all levels of reality, including God himself. And surely, God's representation of reality, the Bible, has been given for the purpose of allowing us to see what mere human observers cannot: the hand of God in the whirlwind.

Relative to the human task of writing our conceptions of ancient Near Eastern history, the traditional approach to the Bible—albeit typically with a good dose of anti-biblical bias—has been to treat it as patient rather than agent. But because the Bible is God's representation of reality, and because the perfections of the true narrative case[151] in

---

150   Hoffmeier, *Israel in Egypt* 40.
151   See Oller and Collins, *Logic of True Narratives*; and Collins and Oller, *Biblical History*.

Scripture are far superior to all other representations, I am convinced by substantial evidence[152] that biblical data must occupy the role of agent in our attempts to reconstruct any sequence of ancient Near Eastern events which overlaps the biblical narrative. Treating the Bible merely as another extant ancient Near Eastern text to be critically considered may lend an air of scholarship to the work of those who deal with biblical subjects, but it is actually the death of true objectivity. The Bible must always be the corrective, never the corrected. If the Bible is God's representation of reality, then an objective assessment of all matters must begin and end with Scripture.

---

152 For example, see K.D. Boa and R.M. Bowman, Jr., *Faith Has Its Reasons* (Colorado Springs: Navpress, 2001); G.R. Habermas, *The Historical Jesus* (Joplin: College Press, 1996); and J.W. Montgomery, *Faith Founded on Fact* (Nashville: T. Nelson, 1978). For a concise, practical presentation of evidential Christian apologetics, see S. Collins, *The Defendable Faith: Lessons in Christian Apologetics* (Albuquerque: Trinity Southwest University Press, 2011).

A Biblically-Adjusted Chronology
of the Eighteenth Dynasty

—⁂—

W hen using historical synchronisms to link the biblical Exodus scenario with a commensurate portion of Eighteenth Dynasty history, I have used only relative dating. Although absolute dating may be more convenient once fixed chronological reference points are established, relative dating is how the ancients understood the timeframes of their world. While we are interested in the linear precision of sequential historical events over long periods of time, ancient Near Eastern chroniclers had no such thing in mind. Their purposes were more immediate, political, religious, and propagandistic, not to mention the fact that their conception of reality was principally cyclical and not linear.

Though the biblical writers used relative dating in the same manner as their Near Eastern counterparts, their overall conception of reality was linear, not cyclical. It can safely be said that the writers of the Old Testament were the first to produce a true conception of history as cause and effect, linear and purposeful.[153] The biblical stories, even in the early books such as Genesis and Exodus, are conceived with the idea that God works in the history of his creation over huge spans of time in which present and future generations are significantly impacted by the events of the past. This is also the idea of history that we "moderns" have adopted.

---

153 See R.K. Harrison, *Old Testament Times* 19-25. Although the history-writing tradition of the Hittites was more linear and objective than the chronicling traditions of Mesopotamia and Egypt, the Hebrews "were by far the best technical writers of history in the Near Eastern antiquity." As Harrison also observes: "Because of the comparative objectivity of the Hebrew records it is possible to employ them as control material in appropriate instances as a means of scaling down the inflated claims of such sources as the Assyrian and Babylonian annals and the occasional Egyptian inscription."

We have done so because the linear, cause-and-effect approach to reality is arguably more scientific. Observably, it is the way the universe works (the permutations of theoretical physics notwithstanding![154]).

How the Hebrews came to adopt such a "scientific" approach to history is a mystery to most scholars. It is difficult to account for the fact that none of Israel's regional neighbors saw reality like they did. The linear idea does not evolve out of the cyclical idea; it must have originated from outside Israel's ancient socio-cultural context.[155] But wherever it came from, it was a radical departure from the Near Eastern norm, and it should give us confidence that the biblical record is, from an historiographical point of view, superior to other ancient Near Eastern records. Therefore, I think it is reasonable to use biblical history to correct the chronological fuzziness of our picture of ancient Egyptian history.

How fuzzy is the absolute chronology of ancient Egypt? From the perspective of absolute dating, pretty fuzzy. Take the Eighteenth Dynasty, for example. Scholars are generally divided into three chronological camps: high, middle, and low (see Table 17). If you follow the high chronology,[156] the Eighteenth Dynasty begins in 1570 BCE (Amosis), places the death of Tuthmosis IV in 1417 BCE, and ends in 1320 BCE (Horemheb). If you hold to the middle chronology,[157] it begins in 1570 BCE (Amosis), places Tuthmosis IV's death in 1386 BCE, and ends in

---

154   See S.W. Hawking, *A Brief History of Time* (New York: Bantam, 1988).
155   If Iron Age Israel did congeal out of the local Canaanite population of the central hill country of Palestine as Finkelstein and Na'aman suggest (see Finkelstein and Na'aman, *Nomadism*), then it seems to me that it would be very difficult to explain how the distinct Israelite conceptions of linear history and rigid monotheism could have evolved out of that context, which was wholly animistic/polytheistic with a local/cyclical view of reality, as was the case throughout the ancient Near East. One need only witness the biblical and archaeological evidence revealing the tenacious affinity of the Israelite populace for pagan Canaanite practices to see just how radical the Hebrew monotheism and world-view actually were. The short-lived nature of the failed quasi-monotheistic reforms of Akhenaten in Egypt accentuate the point. Thus, as I see it, the most reasonable explanation for the existence and success of Israel's "modern" view of history, as well as its unique monotheism, is that the one true God, Yahweh, did in fact reveal these things to the ancient writers of the Hebrew Scriptures.
156   W.C. Hayes, "Chronological Tables (A) Egypt," *CAH*, II.2 (1975) 1038.
157   E. Wente and C. Van Siclen III, "A Chronology of the New Kingdom," in *Studies in Honor of George R. Hughes* (January 12, 1977), *SAOC* 39 (Chicago: The Oriental Institute, 1977) 217-261.

1293 BCE (Horemheb). If you take the low chronology,[158] the Eighteenth Dynasty begins in 1540 BCE (Amosis), puts the death of Tuthmosis IV in 1391 BCE, and ends in 1295 BCE (Horemheb). Other configurations either raise or lower these dates.

Now, I am not suggesting that the biblical chronology provides a complete solution for the Egyptian chronology drift, primarily because the extant versions of the biblical text give us different figures for various chronological features, typically between the Masoretic textual stream and that of the (earlier) Septuagint (LXX).[159] Add to this the fact that the biblical numbers related to the date of the Exodus are most likely rounded approximations, and you can easily see that a perfect fix in terms of absolute chronology is not possible. However, it is possible to use the available biblical dates—derived either from the Masoretic stream or the LXX stream—to adjust the Egyptian chronology slightly in order to increase the chronological precision between the Exodus scenario and the history of the Eighteenth Dynasty and, thus, between the Bible and Egyptian chronology in general. I also remind you that the differences between the biblical dates of the Exodus represented by the Masoretic text and the LXX are along the same order of magnitude as scholars posit for the high, middle, and low chronologies of ancient Egypt. This fact leads me to believe that similar (the same?) chronological phenomena attend both the biblical and Egyptian dating systems, which increases the value of using historical synchronisms to connect the two. Indeed, if they can be connected, we may be able to minimize the drift of both.

If the historical synchronism approach, which I have put forth, reasonably identifies Tuthmosis IV as the Pharaoh of the Exodus—with his death at the time of the Exodus—then adjusting the absolute date of the death of Tuthmosis IV to the date of the Exodus should give us a more accurate depiction of the comprehensive history of the period.[160] If the biblical record is the correct (divine) representation of reality, as I

---

158 K. A. Kitchen, "The Historical Chronology of Ancient Egypt: A Current Assessment," *AA* 67 (1996) 1-13.

159 See Finegan, *Chronology*, for excellent discussions of these kinds of issues.

160 This is a fair exercise regardless of who is proposed as the Pharaoh of the Exodus. But one certainly must consider what both the biblical and Egyptian chronologies will tolerate within their ranges of flexibility.

am convinced, then its integration into our understanding of the history of ancient Egypt will provide a more accurate result than if we rely on Egyptian records alone.

The possible biblical dates for the Exodus are 1446 BCE (MT) and 1406 BCE (LXX)—remember that these are "rounded approximations"— based on the reading of 1 Kings 6:1 (see my discussion in Chapter Two). Thus, the death of Tuthmosis IV would have occurred in one of these two approximate timeframes, neither of which does much damage to the existing chronologies (see Tables 18 and 19). Compared to the high chronology, a 1446 date for the death of Tuthmosis IV would raise the chronology of the Eighteenth Dynasty by about 29 years. Compared to the middle and low chronologies, an upward adjustment of 55 to 60 years would be necessary. Although many scholars wince at such adjustments, most realize that the chronological uncertainties inherent in Egyptian documents could, if necessary, accommodate such revision. For example, if an unequivocal Eighteenth Dynasty reference to an astronomical phenomenon forced scholars into a 1446 BCE date for the death of Tuthmosis IV, then there is ample ambiguity in the regnal data to make such a date work. In other words, given no plausible option, scholars would find a way—although they would pursue numerous avenues!—to make a 1446 date for Tuthmosis IV's death fit. I simply ask the question: If the Masoretic textual stream of 1 Kings 6:1 leading to a 1446 BCE date for the Exodus is of divine intent, then would not that fact be as reliable as the ancient record of an astronomical occurrence? We do not have such an unquestionable piece of astronomical data. We do have the biblical record.

But it is not necessary to approach the issue only from the Masoretic reading of 1 Kings 6:1. As I have also pointed out, the LXX has already proved to provide a superior (correct) reading of Exodus 12:40 (see Appendix Two) regarding the length of the Israelite sojourn in Egypt—215 years, not 430 (MT). If the LXX reading of 1 Kings 6:1 is correct, then the Exodus preceded the fourth year of Solomon's reign by 440 years, not 480, making 1406 the approximate date for the Exodus. With this chronological configuration, the death of Tuthmosis IV would be 1406 BCE, a date close to the average of his death-dates in the high

(1417) and low (1391) chronologies, i.e. 1404 BCE. A terminal date of 1406 BCE for Tuthmosis IV can easily be accommodated within the known chronological uncertainties of the Eighteenth Dynasty.

What I have proposed on the basis of historical synchronisms—that Tuthmosis IV is the Pharaoh of the Exodus—is entirely possible within the range of absolute dating already proposed for that period. For those who take the Bible seriously as a historical document, there will be no problem making such an adjustment. For those whose paradigms disallow the historicity of the Hexateuch, such a revision is still not unreasonable if historical synchronisms between the Exodus narrative and the history of the Eighteenth Dynasty point in that direction.

**The Reigns of the Egyptian Kings of the 18th Dynasty
as Configured in the High (Hayes),
Middle (Wente & Van Siclen),
and Low (Kitchen) Chronologies, BC**

	HIGH CHRONOLOGY	MIDDLE CHRONOLOGY	LOW CHRONOLOGY
Amosis I	(1570-1546)	(1570-1546)	(1540-1515)
Amenhotep I	(1546-1526)	(1551-1524)	(1515-1494)
Tuthmosis I	(1525-1512)	(1524-1518)	(1494-1482)
Tuthmosis II	(1512-1504)	(1518-1504)	(1482-1479)
Hatshepsut	(1503-1482)	(1503/1498-1483)	(1479-1457)
Tuthmosis III	(1504-1450)	(1504-1450)	(1479-1425)
Amenhotep II	(1450-1425)	(1453-1419)	(1427-1401)
Tuthmosis IV	(1425-1417)	(1419-1386)	(1401-1391)
Amenhotep III	(1417-1379)	(1386-1349)	(1391-1353)
Amenhotep IV (Akhenaten)	(1379-1362)	(1350-1334)	(1353-1337)
Smenkhkare	(1364-1361)	(1336-1334)	(1337-1336)
Tutankhamun	(1361-1352)	(1334-1325)	(1336-1327)
Ay	(1352-1348)	(1324-1321)	(1327-1323)
Horemheb	(1348-1320)	(1321-1293)	(1323-1295)

Table 17.

A Biblically-Adjusted Chronology of Egypt's 18th Dynasty
(Using Briggs Weighted-Average Regnal Lengths)
Based on a 1446 BC (Masoretic) Date for the Exodus as the
Death-Year of Tuthmosis IV, Compared with the
High Chronology (Hayes) and Low Chronology (Kitchen)

	HIGH CHRONOLOGY	BIBLICALLY-ADJUSTED CHRONOLOGY	LOW CHRONOLOGY
Amosis I	(1570-1546)	(1604-1580)	(1540-1515)
Amenhotep I	(1546-1526)	(1580-1559)	(1515-1494)
Tuthmosis I	(1525-1512)	(1559-1547)	(1494-1482)
Tuthmosis II	(1512-1504)	(1547-1537)	(1482-1479)
Hatshepsut	(1503-1482)	(1537-1516)	(1479-1457)
Tuthmosis III	(1504-1450)	(1537-1483)	(1479-1425)
Amenhotep II	(1450-1425)	(1483-1457)	(1427-1401)
Tuthmosis IV	(1425-1417)	(1457-1446)	(1401-1391)
Amenhotep III	(1417-1379)	(1446-1408)	(1391-1353)
Amenhotep IV (Akhenaten)	(1379-1362)	(1408-1391)	(1353-1337)
Smenkhkare	(1364-1361)	(1391-1389)	(1337-1336)
Tutankhamun	(1361-1352)	(1389-1380)	(1336-1327)
Ay	(1352-1348)	(1380-1376)	(1327-1323)
Horemheb	(1348-1320)	(1376-1348)	(1323-1295)

Table 18.

**A Biblically-Adjusted Chronology of Egypt's 18th Dynasty
(Using Briggs Weighted-Average Regnal Lengths)
Based on a 1406 BC (LXX) Date for the Exodus as the
Death-Year of Tuthmosis IV, Compared with the
High Chronology (Hayes) and Low Chronology (Kitchen)**

	HIGH CHRONOLOGY	BIBLICALLY-ADJUSTED CHRONOLOGY	LOW CHRONOLOGY
Amosis I	(1570-1546)	(1564-1540)	(1540-1515)
Amenhotep I	(1546-1526)	(1540-1519)	(1515-1494)
Tuthmosis I	(1525-1512)	(1519-1507)	(1494-1482)
Tuthmosis II	(1512-1504)	(1507-1497)	(1482-1479)
Hatshepsut	(1503-1482)	(1497-1476)	(1479-1457)
Tuthmosis III	(1504-1450)	(1497-1443)	(1479-1425)
Amenhotep II	(1450-1425)	(1443-1417)	(1427-1401)
Tuthmosis IV	(1425-1417)	(1417-1406)	(1401-1391)
Amenhotep III	(1417-1379)	(1406-1368)	(1391-1353)
Amenhotep IV (Akhenaten)	(1379-1362)	(1368-1351)	(1353-1337)
Smenkhkare	(1364-1361)	(1351-1349)	(1337-1336)
Tutankhamun	(1361-1352)	(1349-1340)	(1336-1327)
Ay	(1352-1348)	(1340-1336)	(1327-1323)
Horemheb	(1348-1320)	(1336-1308)	(1323-1295)

Table 19.

How Low Did the Once Great Eighteenth Dynasty Sink?

—◊◊◊—

Q. Can we legitimately blame the decline and fall of the Tuthmosid Empire on the biblical Exodus events?...and...Just how low did the once-great Eighteenth Dynasty sink?

A. Yes...and...Things couldn't have gotten any worse for the Boys from Thebes.

At its height, the Egyptian Empire of the Eighteenth Dynasty was without peer in the ancient world. Egypt had never before attained such wealth and influence, and it would never again reach that level of regional domination for the balance of its history. Amosis had driven the hated Hyksos out of Lower Egypt and re-unified the kingdom under Theban rule. Amenhotep I, Tuthmosis I, Tuthmosis II and the intriguing Hatshepsut had successively orchestrated the internal stability that allowed Egypt to flex its muscles both southward into Nubia and northward into Canaan and Syria. During the reigns of the next three Pharaohs—the mighty father-son-grandson dynasts, Tuthmosis III, Amenhotep II, and Tuthmosis IV—the Egyptian realm surged to its greatest expanse, from far south in Nubian Africa northward to the River Euphrates in the hinterlands of western Asia.

But after 158 years of empire-building, the Eighteenth Dynasty entered a bizarre, sixty-year period of implosion, seemingly slow at first, but ever-accelerating toward ultimate collapse. After the untimely death of Tuthmosis IV, who ruled only about eight to ten years,[161] the two ensuing kings—Amenhotep III and Amenhotep IV (Akhenaten)—allowed Egyptian hegemony in Asia to slip away, and the loss of Egypt's Levantine territories seems not to have been gradual. There is little doubt among Egyptological scholars that the last significant Eighteenth Dynasty military foray into Canaan and Syria was during the reign of Tuthmosis IV. We have clear evidence from the last quarter of Amenhotep III's reign—recorded in the Amarna Correspondence—that pro-Egyptian Canaanite and Syrian princes in the Levant were deeply concerned about upheaval in the region and were crying out for at least a minimal level of military support from their once-formidable Nilotic overlords, which, interestingly, never materialized. Additionally, Hittite aggression was mounting against the Mesopotamian kingdom of Mittani, whose rulers had been, since the days of Tuthmosis IV, the "brother" of Pharaoh. Things got even worse in Canaan and Syria during the shaky reign of Akhenaten (as I have documented in the body of this monograph). The fact remains that Egypt either would not, or could not, respond with military assistance to the rapidly deteriorating situation in its now-former Asian provinces.

How did this scenario come about? We are all familiar with the rise and fall of nations and empires—indeed, they all meet their ruin sooner or later for a variety of reasons. So why should we be surprised at the collapse of Egypt's Eighteenth Dynasty? *The oddity is in the timing.* From the days of Tuthmosis III, through the reigns of Amenhotep II and Tuthmosis IV, it is difficult to find any chinks whatsoever in the Egyptian armor. When Tuthmosis IV's son, Amenhotep III, ascended to the throne, he was a little too young to assume full responsibilities, but his mother, Mutemwiya, and possibly others in the royal family, were there to ensure stability (this was not uncommon—remember Hatshepsut!). The Egyptian-Mittanian brotherhood alliance was firmly intact, keeping Hittite aggression in check. The empire was wildly

---

161   K.A. Kitchen, "Ancient Egyptian Chronology for Aegeanists," *MAA*, 2/2 (2002) 9. Professor Kitchen has consistently argued for a short reign (no more than ten years) for Tuthmosis IV. This is a recent exclamation point on the issue. Of course, he is absolutely correct. There are, he states, "no solid grounds whatever for more!" Those who like to "pad" the Eighteenth Dynasty by adding years (even decades!) to the reign of Tuthmosis IV are simply fooling themselves.

wealthy and unchallenged militarily. Three generations of powerful and extremely able pharaohs had given Amenhotep III every opportunity to carry on with the Eighteenth Dynasty program of Nubian and Levantine domination. It is unimaginable that both Amenhotep III and his son, Akhenaten, would not have done everything within the capabilities of Egyptian power and influence to maintain the empire.

But in spite of immediate outward appearances and inherited expectations, the disintegration of Egypt's position in the Near East *did* begin during the reign of Amenhotep III and continued unchecked until the collapse of the Tuthmosid Eighteenth Dynasty shortly after the reign of Akhenaten (see Chapter Five). For reasons not visible to the modern observer, Egypt became strangely powerless to retain its traditional Levantine holdings. It allowed its critically important Mittani alliance to erode for lack of attention. It watched helplessly as Suppiluliuma, the Hittite warrior-king, advanced into what had long been Egyptian territory in Syria. It stood by as the Hittites obliterated the Mittani Kingdom (Pharaoh's "brother"!), resulting in the independence and rise to power of Assyria (a former Mittanian province in central Mesopotamia). Egypt exercised an out-of-character non-involvement as Canaan foamed into chaos. By the time of Tuthmosis IV's death, Egypt had been the ancient Near East's dominant power for well over a century. By the end of Akhenaten's reign, Egypt had slipped to a distant third position behind Hatti and Assyria.

This period of Egyptian history, from the death of Tuthmosis IV to the end of the Eighteenth Dynasty when Horemheb usurped the throne, is generally known as the Amarna Age (named for the royal archive discovered at Tell el-Amarna in Egypt). While many scholars have mistakenly presented the era as one of Egypt's finest hours, there is simply no evidence to support such a conception.[162] Quite the contrary is true. Although Egypt tried to present its best face to the world in typical propagandistic fashion, things were actually going very, very badly. Just how bad did it get? There are many indicators that reveal the lamentable state of affairs in Egypt during the Amarna Age,[163] but there is one

---

162   See Redford, *Akhenaten*.
163   See my discussions in Chapters Five, Six, and Seven of this monograph.

astoundingly bizarre event demonstrating that Egypt—regardless of its Spartan posturing—had slipped dangerously close to complete internal collapse and possible foreign domination. The story is complicated, but I will do my best to summarize the essential elements.

Pharaoh Akhenaten died after a seventeen-year reign, the last two years of which his protégé, Smenkhkare (a cousin, nephew, or bastard son of Akhenaten?[164]), served as co-regent. Smenkhkare died shortly thereafter, leaving the kingdom to another Tuthmosid relative, Tutankhamun, who inherited the throne at only nine years of age. Tutankhamun was likely "bewildered"[165] by the prospect of ruling a faltering Egypt. In the background, two military leaders were closely eyeing the situation: the old general, Ay, and a young, aggressive lieutenant-general named Horemheb.[166] It is entirely probable that the power-base in Egypt, for all intents and purposes, had already passed into the hands of the military. That was certainly the case when Tutankhamun died after a short reign of only nine years. At that point, events took a remarkable twist and turn.

General Ay immediately seized the Egyptian throne. Or did he? Tutankhamun's widow, Ankhesenamun, certainly had other designs. D.B. Redford observes that

> ...Ankhesenamun...did not approve of the new configuration of power. In spite of Ay's formal assumption of pharaonic rule, the bereaved queen seems not to have been suppressed and continued to enjoy a certain freedom of action. In fact, in a formal sense only, graphic art at times even united her with Ay as his consort, a union belied by the gross disparity in their ages, perhaps as much as forty years! There can be no doubt that Ankhesenamun had little use for Ay...Clearly Ankhesenamun had not in any way relinquished the rights to political power she felt was hers. But now she lacked a party of support within her own country, so thoroughly had the [Tuthmosid Eighteenth] dynasty to which she belonged been discredited; and any assistance would have to come from abroad.[167]

---

164 Redford, *Akhenaten* 192-193.
165 Ibid. 215.
166 See Grimal, *History* 241-244.
167 Redford, *Akhenaten* 217.

Thus, Ankhesenamun pursued a course of action unprecedented in Egyptian history: she invited a foreign power to assume the throne of Egypt! But not just *any* foreign power.

Recall that during the reigns of the principal Amarna Period pharaohs, Amenhotep III and Akhenaten, Egypt had lost control of its Asiatic territories in Canaan and Syria, allowing its relationship with, and support of, the Mittani Kingdom—guardian of Egypt's traditional Euphrates border and Syrian interests—to slip into oblivion. Amenhotep III's and Akhenaten's failures[168] had opened the door to Hittite aggression against Mittani and throughout Syria. Well before the time of Tutankhamun's death, the Hittites had crushed Mittani into the dust and had pressed their interests southward to the mountains of Lebanon. Because of Egypt's "brotherhood" alliance with Mittani, which had effectively prevented Hatti from acquiring important Mediterranean access through Syrian coastal cities, the Hittites had become the sworn enemy of both Egypt and Mittani. But now that Mittani was essentially nonexistent and Egypt's Eighteenth Dynasty was teetering on collapse, the Hittite Empire was sitting pretty.

As Ankhesenamun viewed her situation, she concluded that Ay's attempt to wrest the throne of Egypt from the Tuthmosid bloodline—an action no doubt supported by Horemheb who, we find out later, loathed the Amarna pharaohs—was intolerable. And so she appealed to the Hittite king, Suppiluliuma. Her amazing correspondence is recorded in Hittite records:

> My husband has died. I do not have a son. But they say you have many sons. If you would give me one of your sons, he would become my husband. I shall never pick out a servant of mine and make him my husband...I am afraid![169]

Suppiluliuma was flabbergasted and suspicious. Upon reading the letter from Ankhesenamun, he exclaimed, "Such a thing has never

---

168 The failure may not rest entirely, or even partly, on their shoulders. They simply may have been the unfortunate heirs of trouble: the aftermath of what I call the Exodus core events.

169 H.G. Güterbock, "The Deeds of Suppiluliuma as told by his son Mursilis II," *JCS* 10 (1956) 93. I have contemporized somewhat the language from Güterbock's translation.

happened before in my whole life!"[170] Indeed. He had just been invited to place one of his sons on the Egyptian throne, which would have made Egypt a vassal state in the Hittite Empire! Was it a trick? Was it for real? More than a little intrigued, he sent a representative to Egypt to find out if the offer was legitimate. His emissary soon returned with one of Ankhesenamun's ambassadors in tow, along with another letter from the Egyptian queen, revealing her irritation in the face of Suppiluliuma's skepticism:

> Why did you say, "They may deceive me" in that way? If I had had a son, would I have written about my own and my country's shame to a foreign land? You did not believe me... He who was my husband had died. I do not have a son. Never shall I take a servant of mine and make him my husband. I have written to no other country...so give me one of your sons: he will be a husband to me, but in Egypt he shall be king![171]

Finally, Suppiluliuma granted Ankhesenamun her wish, and sent one of his sons, Zidanza, to Egypt. But as soon as the Hittite prince crossed the border into Egypt, he was murdered. The deed was probably carried out at the order of Ay or Horemheb, or both, but the Egyptian records are mute as to the perpetrators. Ankhesenamun also disappeared from the scene.

Needless to say, Suppiluliuma was enraged when the news reached him. Immediately he signaled a military action against Egypt, initially against Egyptian footholds in anti-Lebanon[172] and then, no doubt, against Egypt itself. But suddenly, another bizarre twist entered the picture. Evidently, Egypt had been suffering from some sort of plague off and on throughout the Amarna Period.[173] The plague was possibly transmitted to the Hittites by the Egyptian entourage sent earlier to Hatti by Ankhesenamun. Or perhaps the Hittite army contracted it through their encounters with Egyptian troops. No one really knows. But what

---

170 Ibid.
171 Ibid.
172 The Egyptian military had re-established a presence in Canaan during the reign of Tutankha-mun, under the leadership of generals Ay and Horemheb.
173 Bryce, *Hittites* 198; See also Giles, *Amarna Age* 347-348.

the Egyptian army could not do in the face of the Hittite onslaught, the plague accomplished with great effect: the Hittite hordes were stopped dead in their tracks before they could traverse Canaan en route to Egypt. So, as far as the Hittite/Egyptian conflict was concerned, Egypt, on the one hand, had been neutralized by its internal difficulties, and now Hatti, on the other hand, succumbed to an invisible foe—a plague—that not only neutralized its armies, but even threatened to decimate the Hittite homeland in eastern Asia Minor. It was a virtual stalemate that would eventually result in a treaty between Egypt and Hatti during the Nineteenth Dynasty.

And now back to my original questions: What circumstances converged to create such a scenario? Why did the powerful Tuthmosid Dynasty crumble into oblivion? What would cause the internal affairs of Egypt to deteriorate so completely that a sonless, widowed queen would invite a foreign (enemy!) king to make his son Pharaoh of the Black Land?[174] Bizarre? Yes; but reality nonetheless. Yet, I think there is a perfect explanation for the demise of the Eighteenth Dynasty: the five core events of the Exodus narrative that, according to the biblical accounts, wreaked havoc in Lower Egypt—plagues, plundering, huge labor losses, severe military losses, and the death of Pharaoh himself (Tuthmosis IV). Regardless of its level of power and wealth, such occurrences would have sent Egypt into the kind of crisis situation described in the ancient records. And is it possible that the plagues suffered by Egypt during the Amarna Age (a strain of "plague"? influenza? smallpox?), and subsequently contracted by the Hittites, were the epidemic result of lingering and/or mutating pathogens carried over from the plagues of the Exodus story? Not only is it possible, but I think it is highly probable.

Only in the most dire circumstances possible would the widowed queen of a once-mighty Egyptian dynasty offer Egypt's throne to its most formidable enemy. But it happened—and the Bible tells us why. The Exodus eyewitness, Moses, knew all along the severity of Yahweh's

---

174   The "Black Land" was ancient Egypt's name for itself.

hand against Pharaoh and all his house.[175] Therefore, it should not surprise us that the Tuthmosid Dynasty ultimately met its end as a result of collateral damage from the wrath of God delivered in the final days of Tuthmosis IV's reign.

---

175   The term "pharaoh" means "great house."

The Home of the Canaanites, Hittites, Amorites:

Is Yahweh's Promise a Significant Historical Synchronism?

—⚹—

In multiple passages in the Hexateuch, Yahweh promised that the Israelites, the descendents of Abraham the Hebrew, would inherit "a land flowing with milk and honey" (Ex 3:8)—a Promised Land occupied by three major groups of people: Canaanites, Hittites, and Amorites. That biblical Canaan, "from the river of Egypt to the great river, the Euphrates" (Gen 15:8), was occupied by a people generally known as Canaanites and Amorites, among others, is well known and documented through the Bronze Age. But this swath of the Levant was not "home" to the Hittites until Late Bronze II, a fact that may serve to specify a historical window for the entrance of Joshua and the Israelites into Canaan. Coupled with the fact that the multiple biblical lists of occupants of the Promised Land never include an Egyptian presence, a timeframe for Joshua's conquest of Canaan is perhaps narrower still. It was an Egyptian-less land with a significant Hittite presence that Yahweh promised to deliver into Israelite hands, and this scenario fits uniquely into a rather narrow time-slot during the 14th century BCE.

Two biblical facts support the idea that Israel's Promised Land at the time of the Conquest was not "home" to the Egyptians: (a) Egyptians are never included in any people lists for the land of Canaan; and (b) at no point during the narrative of the book of Joshua do the invading

Israelites ever encounter Egyptians or Egyptian troops. Indeed, it was an Egyptian-less land that God promised them. Of course, both the early (15th century BCE) and late (13th century BCE) dates for the Exodus and Conquest fall during the Late Bronze Age, a time corresponding to the Egyptian New Kingdom Period, and noted for Egypt's domination of Canaan and Syria. Most of the Eighteenth and Nineteenth Dynasty kings pressed their interests into the Levant. Notable pharaohs who exerted hegemony over significant portions of the Levant, particularly Canaan, include Tuthmosis I, II, and III, Amenhotep II, and Tuthmosis IV of the Eighteenth Dynasty, and Seti I, Rameses II, and Merneptah of the Nineteenth Dynasty.

Once Ahmosis, first king of the Eighteenth Dynasty, had driven the hated Hyksos from Lower Egypt, it didn't take long for the soon-to-come Tuthmosid bloodline to pursue imperial expansion northward to the Euphrates River. The height of Egyptian hegemony and presence in Canaan and Syria occurred during the 15th century BCE during the reigns of Tuthmosis III, Amenhotep II, and Tuthmosis IV—a father-son-grandson sequence that prided itself in its Euphrates northern border. The final stage of Egypt's Levantine domination, and the peak of their strength in Asia, occurred during the reign of Tuthmosis IV when he succeeded in making a treaty with Artatama, king of Mittani (northern Mesopotamia). The Mittani king was now guardian and guarantor of Egypt's Euphrates border, while combined Egyptian and Mittani strength secured Mittani's corridor to the Mediterranean through northern Syria. It was a perfect setup for both "brothers." However enraged the Hittites were by this "snub" from Egypt (Mittani was a perennial enemy of the Hittites), there was nothing Hatti could do to pursue its interests in acquiring a Mediterranean corridor of its own in the face of the new Egypto-Mittanian alliance. For the meantime, the Hittites were just sadly out of luck.

Thus, from the late 16th century BCE down to about 1406 BCE (a good "average" date for the end of Tuthmosis IV's reign) the following occurred: (a) Egypt dominated Canaan and Syria to the Euphrates—biblical Canaan; and (b) the Hittites were completely excluded from the Levant. Biblically speaking, down to the end of the 15th century BCE, the Promised Land was dominated by the Egyptian hegemony, and the Hittites were politically and militarily absent. Therefore, through the end of the 15th century BCE, it would have been impossible for Joshua and the Israelites to have waged a conquest campaign against an Egyptian-less land in which Hittites were ensconced. The historical circumstances were not in place through which Yahweh's promises to Israel could be realized with any level of precision.

One might object by observing that there were Hittites in Canaan even before the time of Joshua (Gen 15:20; 23). However, both textually and archaeologically, the Hittites of Abraham's day were probably only "sons of Het" (בני-חת) who came to the Levant as isolated Anatolian immigrants and did not constitute a political or "people group" presence of any consequence. The archaeological record supports this general absence of Anatolian peoples in the Levant, but does affirm that some families did, indeed, immigrate to Canaan (such as the isolated Khirbet Kerak Ware potters of the Galilee during EB III). The fact of the matter is that if Joshua and the Israelites had crossed the Jordan River into Canaan anytime during the 15th century BCE, they would have faced formidable Egyptian resistance, and the Hittite presence would have been nowhere to be found. Through the end of the 15th century BCE, Egypt kept a tight grip on Canaan and Syria, while Mittani, and later the Egypto-Mittanian alliance, effectively locked the Hittites out of the region. But this historical situation would soon undergo a dramatic change.

After the death of Tuthmosis IV, whose reign marked the height of Egyptian supremacy and prestige in the Near East, the sun set rather quickly on the Golden Empire. Why Egyptian records have skirted, with profound silence, the reign of Amenhotep III remains an enigma. Although the mightiest kingdom on earth had passed into his hands, Amenhotep seemed illequipped and, worse, unwilling or unable to maintain the vast empire carved out during the previous century of great, even magnificent, Tuthmosid pharaohs. He had inherited an Egypt with a now-traditional northern border at the Euphrates and reaching five cataracts of the Nile southward into Africa. But it seems that Amenhotep had little or no taste for the domination of foreign lands, and his policies regarding the maintenance of the Asiatic provinces, in particular, were, for all intents and purposes, nonexistent. In short, for some mysterious reason, the Egypt of Amenhotep III shrank back within its pre-imperial borders, while marshalling vast amounts of wealth for internal building projects and bolstering its image of opulence—as if to say, "So what if we no longer have the wherewithal to maintain imperial traditions, we're doing just fine down here…just look around!"

As Amenhotep III, for whatever reasons, turned his back on his father's treaty with Mittani, the great Hittite warrior-king, Suppiluliumma, eyed the deteriorating Egyptian/Mittanian situation with great interest. Without a doubt, the Hittite king remembered the history of how Hatti had been snubbed by Egypt when Tuthmosis IV embraced Mittani instead of Hatti as a northern ally. What Suppiluliumma knew about the internal goings-on in Egypt no one knows for sure. But at least one thing is certain: he knew that it was time to settle an old score with Egypt by attacking Mittani with impunity and, eventually, a few decades later, wiping that Mesopotamian kingdom from the face of the earth. Without hesitation or fear of Egyptian reprisal, Suppiluliumma attacked the Mittani capital, then carved out a long-coveted Hittite corridor to the Mediterranean coast. Hatti marched. Mittani fell. Egypt sat motionless—as paralyzed as the great granite statues Amenhotep III had erected in his own honor.

After Amenhotep died, pharaoh Akhenaten attempted to reverse Egypt's downward spiral by adopting revolutionary religious reforms. The traditional Egyptian gods were replaced by a quasi-monotheism based on the Aten, the sun-disk. The old gods had not protected the Black Land, and it was now threatened with utter collapse. But the Aten proved unequal to the task of restoring the glory of Egypt. The Hittites waxed stronger and were now solidly entrenched in the northern Levant, while the southern Levant writhed in chaos without any hope of assistance from Egypt. Within a few years after Akhenaten's death, Egypt's once-magnificent Eighteenth Dynasty collapsed in what can only be described as embarrassment and disgrace. Then, sometime between 1340 BCE and 1320 BCE (depending on the chronology used), the Egyptian military commander, Horemheb, who longed for the glory-days of the Empire, wrested control of what little remained of the Eighteenth Dynasty and turned Egypt around by the sheer force of his will and administrative skills. Whether pharaoh Horemheb is to be considered the last king of the Eighteenth Dynasty or the first king of the Nineteenth Dynasty is moot. The fact is that Horemheb laid the foundation for the rise of the Nineteenth Dynasty, once again launching military "tours" into the southern Levant and handpicking the first Ramesside pharaoh—an old army buddy, Rameses I. But it was during the reigns of Seti I and Rameses II that Egypt experienced renewed vigor and reasserted its military might in the southern Levant. However, the Hittites continued their presence in the northern Levant until the collapse of their empire about 1205 BCE.

Thus, it is within the terminal parameters of: (a) Egypt's absence from the Levant (ca. 1380-1300 BCE—encompassing both high and low chronologies), and (b) Hatti's domination of the northern Levant during the same period, that the situation in Israel's Promised Land matched the oft-repeated socio-political components expressed and implied by Yahweh himself: "To your descendants I give this land, from the river of Egypt to the great river, the Euphrates—the land of the Hittites,…Amorites, Canaanites…" (Gen 15:18-21); "I have come down to rescue them from the hand of the Egyptians and to bring them up out of that land into a good and spacious land, a land flowing with milk and honey—the home of the Canaanites, Hittites, Amorites…" (Ex 3:8); "I have promised to bring you up out of your misery in Egypt into the land of the Canaanites, Hittites, Amorites…a land flowing with milk and honey" (Ex 3:17); "When Yahweh brings you into the land of the Canaanites, Hittites, Amorites…" (Ex 13:5); "My angel will go ahead of you and bring you into the land of the Amorites, Hittites,… Canaanites…" (Ex 23:23); "I will send an angel before you and drive out the Canaanites, Amorites, Hittites…" (Ex 33:2); "I will drive out before you the Amorites, Canaanites, Hittites…" (Ex 34:11); "Now when the kings west of the Jordan heard about these things—those in the hill country, in the western foothills, and along the entire coast of the Great Sea, as far as Lebanon (the kings of the Hittites, Amorites, Canaanites…)—they came together to make war against Joshua and Israel" (Josh 9:1).

If one puts any credence whatsoever in the accuracy of the biblical description of the land promised to the Israelites, then the Conquest event cannot be reconciled with the time period before the reign of Amenhotep III or after the reign of Horemheb, for Joshua encountered no Egyptian presence in Canaan and was assured that he would not. On the other hand, the Hittites had no controlling presence in the Levant until the latter years of Amenhotep III's reign in the second quarter of the 14th century BCE. Biblically, Joshua and the Israelites entered an Egyptian-less land wherein the Hittites controlled and administered significant territory. And whether one views the biblical record of these data as prophecy and fulfilling history, or simply as history written (accurately!) after the fact, it must be admitted that what the Hebrew Hexateuch describes is a socio-political situation in Canaan that existed for less than fifty years during Egypt's so-called Amarna Period. The convergence of these data effectively rules out the possibility of a Conquest before about 1380 BCE or after 1300 BCE. This seems to be a compelling historical synchronism between ancient Near Eastern history and the biblical record, when both are taken seriously.

BIBLIOGRAPHY

Aharoni, Y. *The Land of the Bible: A Historical Geography*. Philadelphia: Westminster, 1979.

Ahlstrom, G.W. *The History of Ancient Palestine*. Minneapolis: Fortress, 1994.

Aldred, C. *Akhenaten: King of Egypt*. New York: Thames and Hudson, 1988.

Aling, C.F. *A Prosopographical Study of the Reigns of Tuthmosis IV and Amenhotep III*. Doctoral dissertation: University of Minnesota, 1976.

———. *Egypt and Bible History*. Grand Rapids: Baker, 1981.

Anati, A. *Har Karkom: The Mountain of God*. New York: Rizzoli, 1986.

Billington, C.E. "Othniel, Cushan-Rishathaim, and the Date of the Exodus." Paper presented to NEAS, 2001.

Boa, K.D. and R.M. Bowman, Jr. *Faith Has Its Reasons*. Colorado Springs: NavPress, 2001.

Brier, B. *Egyptian Mummies: Unraveling the Secrets of an Ancient Art*. New York: Quill/William Morrow, 1994.

Briggs, P. *Testing the Factuality of the Conquest of Ai Narrative in the Book of Joshua*. Doctoral dissertation. Newburgh: Trinity Theological Seminary, 2001.

Broshi, M. and R. Gophna, "Middle Bronze Age II Palestine: Its Settlements and Population." *BASOR* 261 (1986).

Bryan, B.M. "The Eighteenth Dynasty before the Amarna Period." In I. Shaw (ed.), *OHAE*. New York: Oxford University, 2000.

————. *The Reign of Tuthmosis IV*. Baltimore: Johns Hopkins University, 1991.

Bryce, T. *The Kingdom of the Hittites*. Oxford: Oxford University Press, 1998.

Cate, R. *An Introduction to the Old Testament and its Study*. Nashville: Broadman, 1987.

Collins, S. *The Defendable Faith: Lessons in Christian Apologetics*. Albuquerque: Trinity Southwest University Press, 2011.

Collins, S. and J.W. Oller, Jr. "Is the Bible a True Narrative Representation?" *BRB* I.3 (2001).

Coogan, M.D. "Numeira 1981." *BASOR* 255 (1984).

Crouwel, J.H. and M.A. Littauer, "Chariots." In *OEANE* Vol. 1. New York and Oxford: Oxford University Press, 1997.

Darnell, J.C. and D. Darnell, "1994-95 Annual Report." *The Luxor-Farshut Desert Road Project*. Chicago: Oriental Institute, University of Chicago, 1997.

David, A.R. *The Ancient Egyptians: Religious Beliefs and Practices*. New York and London: Routledge and Kegan Paul, 1982.

Dever, W.G. *What Did the Biblical Writers Know and When Did They Know It?* Grand Rapids/Cambridge, UK: Eerdmans, 2001.

Finegan, J. *Handbook of Biblical Chronology*, rev. ed. Peabody: Hendrickson, 1998.

Finkelstein, I. "From Sherds to History." *IEJ* 48 (1998). Based on a 1996 *Eretz Israel* article by Finkelstein published in Hebrew as "The Settlement History of the Transjordan Plateau in the Light of Survey Data".

Finkelstein, I. and N. Na'aman, eds. *From Nomadism to Monarchy*. Jerusalem: Israel Exploration Society, 1994).

Finkelstein, I. and N.A. Silberman, *The Bible Unearthed: Archaeology's New Vision of Ancient Israel and the Origins of Its Sacred Texts*. New York: Free Press, 2001.

Flavius Josephus, *The Antiquities of the Jews* (2.15.2). In *The Works of Josephus: New Updated Edition*, tr. by W. Whiston. Peabody: Hendrickson, 1987).

Fouts, D.M. *The Use of Large Numbers in the Old Testament*. Doctoral dissertation. Dallas: Dallas Theological Seminary, 1992.

Gardiner, A. *Egypt of the Pharaohs*. London: Oxford University Press, 1961.

Giles, F.J. *The Amarna Age: Western Asia, ACES 5*. Warminster: Aris and Phillips, 1997.

Giveon, R. "Tuthmosis IV and Asia." *JNES* 28.1 (January 1969).

Goetze, A. "The Struggle for the Domination of Syria (1400-1300 B.C.)." *CAH* II.2, 1975.

Gonen, R. "The Late Bronze Age." In A. Ben-Tor (ed.), *The Archaeology of Ancient Israel*. New Haven and London: Yale University, 1992.

Grimal, N. *A History of Egypt*. Oxford: Oxford University, 1992.

Güterbock, H.G. "The Deeds of Suppiluliuma as told by his son Mursilis II." *JCS* 10 (1956).

Habermas, G.R. *The Historical Jesus*. Joplin: College Press, 1996.

Hansen, D.G. *Evidence for Fortifications at Late Bronze I and IIA Locations in Palestine*. Doctoral dissertation. Newburgh: Trinity Theological Seminary, 2000.

Harrison, R.K. *Old Testament Times*. Grand Rapids: Eerdmans, 1970.

Hawking, S.W. *A Brief History of Time*. New York: Bantam, 1988.

Hayes, W.C. "Chronological Tables (A) Egypt." *CAH*, II.2, 1975.

―――. "Egypt: Internal Affairs from Tuthmosis I to the Death of Amenophis III." *CAH* II.1. 1973.

Herzog, C. and M. Gichon. *Battles of the Bible*. London: Greenhill Books, 2002.

Hoerth, A.J. *Archaeology and the Old Testament*. Grand Rapids: Baker, 1998.

Hoffmeier, J.K. "Moses." *ISBE*, G.W. Bromiley, gen. ed. Grand Rapids: Eerdmans, 1986.

―――. *Israel in Egypt: The Evidence for the Authenticity of the Exodus Tradition*. New York/Oxford: Oxford U., 1996.

Hoffner, H.A. "The Hittites and Hurrians." In D.J. Wiseman (ed.), *Peoples of Old Testament* Times. London: Oxford University, 1973.

―――. "The Hittites." In Hoerth, Mattingly, and Yamauchi (eds.), *Peoples of the Old Testament World*. Grand Rapids: Baker, 1994.

James, T.G.H. "From the Expulsion of the Hyksos to Amenophis I." *CAH* II.1,1973.

Kemp, B.J. *Ancient Egypt: Anatomy of a Civilization*. London and New York: Routledge, 1989.

Kitchen, K.A. *Ancient Orient and Old Testament*. Chicago: InterVarsity, 1966.

———. *The Bible in Its World*. Downers Grove: InterVarsity, 1978.

———. *Pharaoh Triumphant: The Life and Times of Ramesses II*. Warminster: Aris and Phillips, 1982.

———. "History of Egypt (chronology)." In D.N. Freedman (ed.), *ABD* Vol. 2. New York: Doubleday, 1992.

———. "The Patriarchal Age: Myth or Mystery." *BAR* 21.2 (1995).

———. "The Historical Chronology of Ancient Egypt: A Current Assessment." *AA* 67 (1996).

———. "The Patriarchs Revisited: A Reply to Dr. Ronald S. Hendel." *NEASB* 43 (1998).

———. "Ancient Egyptian Chronology for Aegeanists." *MAA*, 2/2 (2002).

———. *On the Reliability of the Old Testament*. Grand Rapids/Cambridge, UK: Eerdmans, 2003.

Krahmalkov, C.R. "Exodus Itinerary Confirmed by Egyptian Evidence." *BAR* 20.5 (1994).

Lemche, N.P. *Prelude to Israel's Past*. Peabody: Hendrickson, 1998.

Liverani, M. "The Amorites." In D.J. Wiseman (ed.), *Peoples of Old Testament* Times. London: Oxford University, 1973.

Merrill, E.H. *Kingdom of Priests: A History of Old Testament Israel*. Grand Rapids: Baker, 1987.

Millard, A.R. "The Canaanites." In D.J. Wiseman (ed.), *Peoples of Old Testament Times*. London: Oxford University, 1973.

Miller, J.M. and J.H. Hayes, *A History of Ancient Israel and Judah*. Philadelphia: Westminster, 1986.

Montet, P. *Eternal Egypt*. London: Phoenix, 1964).

Montgomery, J.W. *Faith Founded on Fact*. Nashville: T. Nelson, 1978.

Moorey, P.R.S. "The Emergence of the Light, Horse-Drawn Chariot in the Near East c. 2000-1500 B.C." *WA* 18.2 (1986).

Moran, W.L. *The Amarna Letters*. Baltimore: Johns Hopkins University, 1992.

Murray, M.A. *The Splendor that Was Egypt*. New York: Praeger, 1969.

Na'aman, N. "The 'Conquest of Canaan' in the Book of Joshua and in History." In Finkelstein and Na'aman (eds.), *From Nomadism to Monarchy*. Jerusalem: Israel Exploration Society, 1994.

Naveh, J. *Early History of the Alphabet*, second rev. ed. Jerusalem: Magnes, 1987.

Oaukin, M.A. *Mysteries of the Alphabet*. New York: Abbeyville Press, 1999.

Oller, Jr., J.W. and S. Collins. *The Logic of True Narratives*. *BRB* I.2 (2000).

Pritchard, J.B., ed. "Hymn of Victory of Merneptah (The 'Israel Stela')." *ANET*, third ed. Princeton: Princeton University, 1969.

Ray, Jr., P.J. "The Duration of the Israelite Sojourn in Egypt." *BS* 17.2 (2004). This is the revised version of an article that originally appeared in *AUSS* 24 (1986).

Redford, D.B. *Akhenaten: the Heretic King*. Princeton: Princeton University, 1984.

———. *Egypt, Canaan, and Israel in Ancient Times*. Princeton: Princeton University, 1992.

Reeves, N. *Akhenaten: Egypt's False Prophet*. New York: Thames and Hudson, 2001.

Roux, G. *Ancient Iraq*, third ed. New York: Penguin, 1992.

Schaub, R.T. "Bab edh-Dhra'." In E. Stern (ed.), *NEAEHL*, Vol. 1. Jerusalem and New York: Israel Exploration Society and Carta; Simon and Schuster, 1993.

Schulman, A.R. "Chariots, Chariotry and the Hyksos." *JSSEA* 10 (1980).

Shaw, I. "Egyptian Chronology and the Irish Oak Calibration." *JNES* 44.4 (1985).

———, ed. *OHAE*. New York: Oxford University, 2000.

Shaw, I. and P. Nicholson. "Borders, Frontiers and Limits." *DAE*. London: British Museum, 1995.

———. "History and Historiography." *DAE*. London: British Museum, 1995.

Smend, R. "Mose als geshichtliche Gestalt." *HZ* 260 (1995).

Smith, G.E. *The Royal Mummies*. London: Duckworth, 1912/2000.

Steindorff, G.S. and K.C. Seele. *When Egypt Ruled the East*. Chicago: University of Chicago, 1957.

Thiele, E.R. *The Mysterious Numbers of the Hebrew Kings*. Grand Rapids: Zondervan, 1983.

Traunecker, C. *The Gods of Egypt*. Ithaca and London: Cornell University, 2001.

Van Seters, J. *The Hyksos: A New Investigation*. New Haven: Yale University, 1966.

Waterhouse, S.D. "Who are the Habiru of the Amarna Letters?" *JATS* 12/1 (2001).

Wente, E.F. "Who Was Who Among the Royal Mummies." *The Oriental Institute News and Notes* 144 (1995).

Wente, E. and C. Van Siclen, "A Chronology of the New Kingdom." *SAOC* 39. Chicago: Oriental Institute, 1977.

———. "A Chronology of the New Kingdom." In *Studies in Honor of George R. Hughes* (January 12, 1977), *SAOC* 39. Chicago: The Oriental Institute, 1977.

White, J.E.M. *Ancient Egypt: Its Culture and History*. New York: Dover, 1970.

Wood, B.G. "Did the Israelites Conquer Jericho?" *BAR* 16.2 (1990).

———. "The Walls of Jericho." *BS* 12.2 (1999).

———. "The Discovery of the Sin Cities of Sodom and Gomorrah." *BS* 12.3 (1999).

———. "Khirbet el-Maqatir, 1995-1998." *IEJ* 50.1-2 (2000).

———. "Khirbet el-Maqatir, 1999." *IEJ* 50.3-4 (2000).

———. "Khirbet el-Maqatir, 2000." *IEJ* 51.2 (2001).

Zuhdi, O. "Dating the Exodus: A Study in Egyptian Chronology." *KMT* 4.2 (1993).

Made in the USA
Middletown, DE
06 September 2021